THE
BRITISH & IRISH
LIONS
MISCELLANY

THE LIONS

THE
BRITISH & IRISH
LIONS
MISCELLANY

THE LIONS

BY RICHARD BATH

VSP

Vision Sports Publishing
2 Coombe Gardens
London
SW20 0QU

www.visionsp.co.uk

Published by Vision Sports Publishing, 2008

ISBN 13: 978-1-905326-34-1

Official WebSite of the British & Irish Lions: www.lionsrugby.com

Statistcs: Stuart Farmer Media Services
Illustrations: Bob Bond
Kit illustrations: Anne Cakebread

Typeset by Palimpsest Book Production Limited, Grangemouth, Stirlingshire

Printed and bound in Germany by GGP Media GmbH, Pössneck

— AUTHOR'S NOTE —

Although the Lions weren't truly representative of all four home unions until 1910 and weren't called 'the Lions' until 1924 at the earliest, I have used the term to describe all combined touring teams from the British Isles, starting with the 1888 team. All statistics were compiled on that basis, and include the tours to Argentina, which are classified as official tours and for which Argentina awarded caps.

Similarly, although New Zealand weren't referred to as the 'All Blacks' until the Originals tour of Britain in 1905 and South Africa weren't called the 'Springboks' until the side captained by Paul Roos toured Britain in 1906, I have occasionally used the term to describe their national sides before that point. Again, it was primarily for ease of reference.

Although their Sunday name is The British Isles Rugby Union Team and they are often colloquially (and wrongly) referred to as the British Lions (or, latterly, by the full official title of The British & Irish Lions), for ease of reference I have used the term 'the Lions' throughout this book. Any use of the term Britain or British Isles in the context of the Lions is simply a geographical term to describe these islands.

I have leant heavily upon the expertise of Jim Telfer and others when compiling the Lions Greatest XV, but ultimately the choice was mine. The only pre-requisite for selection was that I had to have seen each player at first hand, or know someone who has. Therefore, all the players in the team are post-war players.

There are more than 30 books on the Lions which are all worth a read, but if your interest in Lions history has been piqued, the best starting points are Clem Thomas's *The History of the British & Irish Lions*, Ron Palenski's *All Blacks v Lions*, and John Griffith's *British Lions*. The official website of the Lions is www.lionsrugby.com.

Finally I'd like to thank Jim Drewett at Vision Sports Publishing and statistician Stuart Farmer for their time and expertise in the compilation of this book. I hope there are no mistakes, but if you find one please do let us know and we will rectify for future editions.

For the purposes of this book I have used the scoring system in use at the time a game was played, as opposed to converting the score to the modern-day equivalent. The list overleaf shows a time-line for the various changes to the scoring system.

1881: Various (see *Nightmare for Stats Men*, page 107)

1891: Try 2pts; Penalty 3pts; converted try 5pts; drop goal or goal from a mark 4pts

1894: try 3pts; penalty 3pts; converted try 5pts; drop goal or goal from a mark 4pts

1905: Try 3pts; converted try 5pts; drop goal 4pts; drop goal or penalty 3pts

1948: Try 3pts; converted try 5pts; penalty 3pts; drop goal 3pts

1972: Try 4pts; converted try 6pts; penalty 3pts; drop goal 3pts

1992: Try 5pts; converted try 7pts; penalty 3pts; drop goal 3pts

Richard Bath
Ayrshire, 2007
rbath@scotsman.com

Every effort has been made to ensure the accuracy of the information supplied on these pages. However, should you notice any errors or oversights in *The British & Irish Lions Miscellany* please contact us and we will amend for future editions.

Please write to:
British & Irish Lions Miscellany
Vision Sports Publishing
2 Coombe Gardens
London
SW20 0QU

Or e-mail:
corrections@visionsp.co.uk

— THE BIRTH OF THE LIONS —

The Lions rugby union team is drawn from the best players in England, Ireland, Wales and Scotland and is the oldest and most famous touring team still in existence in the sporting world.

In 1888, sporting entrepreneurs Alfred Shaw and Arthur Shrewsbury, who had already successfully staged a cricket tour to Australia, approached the Rugby Football Union for permission to put together a similar touring side for rugby. The RFU had no interest in getting involved, but allowed Shaw and Shrewsbury to go ahead as long as the players were not paid. A team was hastily assembled, set off for Australia and New Zealand, and although this team was not called 'the Lions', it is widely held to be the birth of the British and Irish team we now call the Lions.

Indeed, these tours took many guises, including an Anglo-Welsh tour to Australia in 1908, before the British Isles Rugby Union Team (BIRUT for short) earned its more familiar modern moniker. That happened in 1924, in fact, when the team arrived in South Africa with a lion motif on their ties, and the local press and public began referring to the team as 'the Lions'.

The name quickly caught on, although following the partitioning of Ireland official guidance stressed that the team was not to be known as the 'British Lions', or even 'the British & Irish Lions', but simply as 'the Lions' (in the same way that the All Blacks are never 'the New Zealand All Blacks', the Wallabies are never 'the Australian Wallabies' and the Boks are never 'the South African Springboks').

During their 1930 tour of New Zealand and Australia, the side wore dark blue jerseys with three gold lions emblazoned on the front and, following the lead of Cliff Porter's 1924–25 All Black 'Invincibles', who distributed silver fern lapel badges on their tour of Britain, the tourists handed out gold-plated lion pin badges to friends and schoolchildren in New Zealand.

By the end of the tour the legend of the Lions had been sealed in sporting legend.

— THE LIONS ON TOUR: 1888
(NEW ZEALAND & AUSTRALIA) —

In Australia: P16, W14, D2, Pts 211–66
In New Zealand: P19, W13, L2, D4, Pts 82–33
No tests

Once Australian-based sporting promoters Alfred Shaw and Arthur Shrewsbury had been given permission by the RFU to run an overseas tour by a British rugby team, they contacted an agent in England and immediately set about putting together a squad.

This was essentially a commercial enterprise (ironically, considering the RFU were so concerned that the players should not be paid) so there was no concerted attempt to include all four home nations and the squad of players was drawn primarily from the dominant northern clubs plus three from Hawick, although Irish-born Arthur Paul and Welshman William Thomas were included.

The side was captained by Bob Seddon of Swinton and Lancashire until he drowned in a boating accident on the Hunter River near Maitland (see *Tour of Tragedy*, page 70), at which stage Andrew Stoddart, the former England cricket captain, took over.

The 22-man team played an incredible 35 rugby matches in five months, drawing six and losing just two (both in New Zealand), as well as 19 Victoria Rules (Aussie Rules) games. Often matches would be played on consecutive days, and it says much for Swinton forward Harry Eagles that he played in all 54 matches. The star of the side, though, was dashing threequarter John Nolan.

Against all expectations, the shorter New Zealand leg was by far the hardest part of the tour, but there were no tests. The seed of something great, however, had been sown.

Backs: Fullbacks: JT Haslam (Batley), AG Paul (Swinton) Centres and wings: J Anderton (Salford), Dr H Brooks (Edinburgh Univ), HC Speakman (Runcorn), AE Stoddart (Blackheath and England, made captain after RL Sedden drowned on tour) Fly-halves and scrum-halves: W Bumby (Swinton), W Burnet (Hawick), J Nolan (Rochdale Hornets). **Forwards**: T Banks (Swinton), R Burnet (Hawick), JP Clowes (Halifax), H Eagles (Swinton), T Kent (Salford), C Mathers (Bramley), AP Penketh (Douglas, Isle of Man), RL Seddon (Swinton, capt), DJ Smith (Corinthians, Edinburgh Univ), AJ Stuart (Dewsbury), WH Thomas (Cambridge Univ and Wales), S Williams (Salford). **Managers:** A Shaw and A Shrewsbury.

— A CLOSE SHAVE —

On the 1997 tour of South Africa, English scrum-half Matt Dawson asked bald Irish hooker Keith Wood to clip his hair with the clippers he carried with him. Wood promptly shaved all Dawson's hair off.

— THE BUTTER MAN —

On the 1993 tour of New Zealand, at the team hotel Lions bigwig Bob Weighill asked for an extra pat of butter to accompany his breakfast, but was told he didn't qualify for extra butter privileges. "Do you know who I am?" asked Weighill, before giving the waiter the full rollcall of his titles and jobs. When he had finished, the waiter looked at him. "And do you know who I am?" he asked Weighill. "No," replied the Englishman. "I'm the man in charge of the butter," he replied.

— LIONS RECORDS: MOST TRIES IN TEST MATCHES —

For:

Tries	Name	Tests	Years
6	Tony O'Reilly	10	1955–59
5	JJ Williams	7	1974–77
4	Willie Llewellyn	4	1904
4	Malcolm Price	5	1959

Against:

Tries	Name	Country	Games	Years
5	Frank Mitchinson	New Zealand	3	1908
5	Theuns Briers	South Africa	4	1955
4	Tom van Vollenhoven	South Africa	4	1955
4	Ralph Caulton	New Zealand	3	1959
4	Stu Wilson	New Zealand	4	1983

— GREATEST LIONS XV: JEFF BUTTERFIELD (OUTSIDE CENTRE) —

Jeff Butterfield

The South Africans had never before encountered a player like English centre Jeff Butterfield. Part piano-mover, part concert pianist, he was as comfortable gliding around opponents as he was running over the top of them. He was the perfect mix of those two great Lions, Guscott and Gibbs.

In 1955 his mix of physicality, aggression, pace and sleight of hand were key components in fashioning a free-running side that Springbok legend and then SARU President Danie Craven described as the best ever to tour South Africa. Not only was the outside centre the 1955 side's top try-scorer in tests, scoring in the first, second and third tests – he also scored on his debut for England and for the Lions – but he was a prolific provider of tries for his wings. The 1955 Lions scored a record number of tries in South Africa, and he provided a high proportion of them.

Butterfield – or "Buttercup" as Cliff Morgan used to call him – was fortunate to be paired alongside another centre with similar attributes in England's Phil Davies. Together, their aggressive lines of running, shrewd reading of the game and formidable defence had the South Africans continually on the back foot.

Nowhere was this more obvious than in the tests, where Butterfield was arguably the single most important player in a series often described as the best the Lions have ever been involved in. A big-game player, in the epic first test won by a single point, his brilliant linking play broke the deadlock when he took a pass from Davies behind his ear and drew fullback Jack van der Schyff before putting Cecil Pedlow away for a try with one flowing, instinctive movement. Butterfield then displayed his uncanny running abilities when his mazy run took him past several would-be Springbok tacklers and over for the winning try.

Just to prove it was no fluke, Butterfield scored another in the heavy second test defeat, ran 80 yards to score the winning try against Northern Transvaal in one of the hardest games on tour, and then started the 9–6 third test win which put the series beyond the Springboks with an inspired moment of genius when he kicked a left-footed drop-goal – not bad for a right-footed non-kicker who had never kicked a goal before and would never kick one again.

Butterfield also scored a try in that game as he picked up six of the Lions' nine points, the centre barging his way over the line with three helpless Springbok defenders vainly hanging onto his back.

As well as a try-scorer and try-maker of genius, Butterfield also made a crucial contribution to the success of the 1955 Lions by acting as their physical training instructor throughout the tour. It was a role he reprised in New Zealand in 1959 when he again toured with the Lions only to find his appearances highly restricted due to injury.

Butterfield's main competitors for the accolade of greatest Lions outside centre were (in order) Jeremy Guscott, John Dawes, Ian McGeechan, Jack Matthews and Dave Hewitt.

Jeff Butterfield stats
Born 9th August 1929
Toured: 1955 & 1959
Tests: 1955 SA 1, 2, 3, 4
28 caps for England 1953–59
Club: Northampton.

— THE GREATEST LIONS MATCHES: 1 —

New Zealand 3, Lions 6
First test
21st June 1930, Dunedin

Doug Prentice's 1930 Lions lost two successive early games to Canterbury and Wellington, yet the Kiwis began to worry when the tourists beat West Coast/Buller 34–11 and then walloped mighty Otago by the unheard of score of 33–9 the week before the first test. It was a score which had the All Black selectors openly hoping for rain in order to close down the Lions' free-running back division.

They didn't just get rain, but driving sleet and snow on the morning of the match as one of the heaviest snowstorms for many years only abated at half-time. Yet instead of the dour forward battle the conditions would usually dictate, the Dunedin crowd was treated to one of the most exciting tests ever seen in New Zealand.

The Lions got off the mark quickly when shortly after kick-off their influential fly-half Roger Spong kicked crossfield for fellow Englishman Jim Reeve to beat wing George Hart to the ball, the rangy Quins wing then rounding the All Black to claim the opening try. The Lions forwards were in dominant form before the interval, with George Beamish, Ivor Jones and Jimmy Farrell outstanding, and they turned around 3–0 ahead.

The All Blacks, playing in white shirts as the Lions' tops were dark blue, hit back straight after the interval. Hart was the national sprint champion and when he found himself on the end of a sweeping threequarters movement he barrelled over right in the corner to bring the scores back to 3–3, with legendary fullback George Nepia hitting the post with the conversion.

Despite a match of high excitement in terrible conditions, the scores stayed that way until seconds before the final whistle when Welsh flanker Ivor Jones, a player of such immense talent that the New Zealanders dubbed him 'the King' before Barry John was even a twinkle in his father's eye, broke two tackles in his own 25 and hared off up the field. With only Nepia to beat, the flanker drew the fullback, committing him to the tackle before feeding onrushing wing Jack Morley for the winning try.

Not only were the Lions the first team ever to win a test at that previously impregnable Kiwi citadel of Carisbrook, but they were the first Lions side to win the first test of a series in New Zealand. Not until 1971 was another Lions side to match the feat.

— FLOWER OF SCOTLAND —

The first time the Corries' 1960s song Flower of Scotland was ever used in a rugby context wasn't at Murrayfield, or even at a Scotland away game, but by Scottish Lions supporters in New Zealand in 1977. The song became one of the many tour anthems, sung by fans and players alike, even forming part of an album cut by the Lions squad in 1977 (see *Sing-along with the Lions*, page 40).

— LIONS RECORDS: MOST POINTS IN TEST MATCHES —

For:

Pts	Name	Tests	Years
66	Gavin Hastings	6	1989–93
47	Jonny Wilkinson	5	2001–05
44	Phil Bennett	8	1974–77
41	Neil Jenkins	3+1	1997–2001
35	Tom Kiernan	5	1962–68

Against:

Pts	Name	Country	Tests	Years
46	Allan Hewson	New Zealand	4	1983
44	Matt Burke	Australia	2+1	2001
44	Dan Carter	New Zealand	2	2005
39	Don Clarke	New Zealand	4	1959
37	Michael Williment	New Zealand	4	1966
36	Michael Lynagh	Australia	3	1993

— DEREK'S WINNING RUN —

Llanelli skipper Derek Quinnell, the only uncapped player on the 1971 tour of New Zealand, has featured on the winning side against the All Blacks more often than any other British player. Not only did he beat them playing for the 1971 Lions and the 1977 Lions, he also beat them playing for the Barbarians and Llanelli in 1972–73, making four wins in total (one more than either Gareth Edwards or Phil Bennett). Quinnell's first start for Wales was also against New Zealand, although that went less well, Wales losing 19–16 at Cardiff Arms Park in 1972.

— THE LIONS ON TOUR: 1891 (SOUTH AFRICA) —

P20, W20, Pts 226–1
Tests: W4–0 (Port Elizabeth), W3–0 (Kimberley), W4–0 (Cape Town)

The RFU was probably right to suspect that the 1888 tour was tainted by professionalism, so when an invitation arrived from the Western Cape Union accompanied by an undertaking from Cecil Rhodes to underwrite the costs, the Union organised the next tour itself. Instead of the predominantly working-class men of the 1888 tour, this expedition was comprised mainly of Oxbridge men travelling with London Scot Bill Maclagan as skipper and Richmond's establishment man Edwin 'Daddy' Ash as manager.

The tourists were far too experienced for the South Africans, however, and not only did they remain undefeated in their 20 matches, they also won them all while conceding just one point, in the 15–1 win over Cape Town the day after their arrival. Maclagan's side was also the first from the British Isles to play a test, winning the matches in Port Elizabeth (4–0), Kimberley (3–0) and Cape Town (4–0).

Although players such as Maclagan, with his 26 caps for Scotland, were vastly experienced the undoubted star of the show was 6ft 3in 15 stone Blackheath and Cambridge University centre Randolph Aston, whose 30 tries on tour remain a record.

Backs: Fullbacks: E Bromet (Cambridge Univ), WG Mitchell (Richmond and England) Centres and wings: RL Aston (Blackheath and England), PR Clauss (Birkenhead Park and Scotland), WE Maclagan (Edinburgh Acads and Scotland, capt) Fly-halves and scrum-halves: H Marshall (Blackheath and Cambridge Univ), BG Roscoe (Manchester), A Rotherham (Cambridge Univ and England), W Wotherspoon (Cambridge Univ and Scotland).

Forwards: WE Bromet (Richmond and England), JH Gould (Old Leysians), J Hammond (Cambridge Univ), PF Hancock (Blackheath and England), WJ Jackson (Gloucester and Cambridge Univ), RG MacMillan (London Scottish and Scotland), WE Mayfield (Cambridge Univ), CP Simpson (Cambridge Univ), AA Surtees (Harlequins), R Thompson (Cambridge Univ), WH Thomson (Cambridge Univ), T Whittaker (Lancashire).

Manager: E Ash.

— NOW YOU SEE THEM . . . —

Before England played New Zealand in the first test in 1977, a Kiwi journalist asked Bill Beaumont if it worried him that some pundits thought that the All Blacks were invincible. "Of course it does," replied Beaumont in all seriousness. "If we can't see them, how can we beat them?"

— TOUCH JUDGES' SPLIT DECISION —

In the early days of Lions tours, the visiting team supplied one of the two touch judges. When Lions second row Brian Black kicked for goal in the third test in Auckland in 1930, the tourists' man – non-selected Lions captain Doug Prentice – raised his flag for a successful kick, only to be overruled by the other touch judge, Original All Black George Nicholson. In 1959, exactly the opposite happened during the first test at Carisbrook when Lion Mick English, acting as the visiting touch judge, ruled that one of Don Clarke's penalties for New Zealand had missed the left upright, only to find himself overruled by the home touch judge. The penalty stood and New Zealand won 18–17.

— MEADS IS THE MAIN MAN —

With 11 caps over three tours (1959, 1966 and 1971), All Black second row legend Colin Meads has played more tests against the Lions than any other man.

— SNORE DRAWS —

The only 0–0 draws in Lions history were on 15th July 1896 against Western Province, the second test against South Africa in Kimberley in 1903 and on 17th August 1904 when the Lions played a combined Taranaki/Ranganui/Manawatu side in New Plymouth.

— GREATEST LIONS XV: MIKE GIBSON (INSIDE CENTRE) —

Mike Gibson

There is much debate over many of the players in the ultimate Lions team, yet there will be none over Mike Gibson's inclusion. Universally acknowledged as the perfect centre, he maintained the highest standards of play for an incredible 15 years, in the process winning 69 Ireland caps and going on a record-equalling five successive Lions tours.

The Ulsterman mixed an uncanny positional sense and ability to read the game with the raw physical attributes of a top centre and a willingness to work harder than any of his contemporaries to maintain his edge. A virtual teetotaller, when it came to training he had a work ethic that was light years ahead of its time. It was this that helped him maintain a playing career of incredible length.

A player with remarkable judgement and the ability to time a pass to perfection, Gibson specialised in making teammates look good, and had a fabled ability to mould his game to the players around him. That was demonstrated most vividly in 1971, when Gibson was at the height of his powers and combined to telling effect with Barry John at fly-half and captain John Dawes at outside centre.

Gibson thrilled the New Zealand crowds with the timing of his attacking runs and with his all-round footballing ability. That was memorably shown in the second test in 1971 when JPR Williams flung what looked like a hospital pass to Gibson, only for the Irishman to deftly guide the ball on to Gerald Davies, wrongfooting the whole All Blacks defence with his split-second timing.

Previously, Gibson had been one of the few players to emerge from the 1966 Lions tour with any credit, proving himself as adaptable as he was durable. He consolidated that reputation on the 1968 Lions tour to South Africa when he not only stood in at fly-half for the injured Barry John, but also played 11 of the final 13 matches for the injury-ravaged tourists.

Although he went on the 1974 tour, his duties as a lawyer meant he arrived mid-tour after Ian McGeechan and Dick Milliken had already struck up a formidable partnership, and the modest Gibson won yet more friends with the enthusiastic way he embraced the role of understudy. In 1977, he toured with the Lions again but back and hamstring problems meant he was never in contention for a test place.

Gibson's main competitors for the place of inside centre were (in order) Scott Gibbs, Brian O'Driscoll, Bleddyn Williams and Phil Davies.

Mike Gibson stats
Born 3rd December 1942
Toured: 1966, 1968, 1971, 1974, 1977
Tests: 1966 NZ 1, 2, 3, 4; 1968 SA 1 (R), 2, 3, 4; 1971 NZ 1, 2, 3, 4
69 caps for Ireland
Clubs: North of Ireland and Cambridge University.

— WELSH PRIDE —

When it comes to test teams, there has never been a Lions XV that hasn't included at least one Welshman – a record none of the other three nations can match.

The Lions didn't include a single Irishman in the first test in 1904 as well as the second and third tests in 1989, there were no Englishman in five of the six tests of the 1950 tour, no Scots in four of the five tests in 1930 or any of the three tests against the All Blacks in 2005 (only Gordon Bulloch made it into a 22, and then only once, for the third test.

— THE LIONS ON TOUR: 1896 (SOUTH AFRICA) —

P21, W19, L1, D1, Pts 310–45
Tests: W8–0 (Port Elizabeth), W17–8 (Johannesburg),
W9–3 (Kimberley), L0–5 (Cape Town)

The 1896 British Isles Rugby Union Team, the first after the great split that was to create rugby league, was captained by Blackheath and Cambridge forward Johnny Hammond, the vice-captain of the 1891 tour. The side didn't have outstanding backs but contained exceptional forwards, including 6ft 5in Froude 'Baby' Hancock from Somerset, who weighed in at almost 19 stone and had also toured in 1891.

They found that the standard of play in the Cape had improved considerably, and although they were a better side than Maclagan's 1891 outfit and remained unbeaten throughout their non-test matches, winning 16 and drawing 0–0 with Western Province, it was not with the ease of five years earlier as they scored 310 points but conceded 45. Worse still, after conceding two tries in the second test and then having to come from behind in the Third, they became the first Lions to lose a test when Barrie 'Fairy' Heatlie's South Africa won the fourth test 5–0. The key moment in this game came when Fred Byrne fumbled the ball and was tackled by Ferdie Aston (the younger brother of 1891 star Randolph), who dropped the ball for Alf Larard to score the game's only try.

The Lions indulged in the usual social gaiety and rowdiness, which was given a boost by the presence of a significant number of Irish players for the first time. In fact most of the best players were from the Irish team which had won two Championships and a Triple Crown in the preceding three seasons, with halfback Louis Magee, 17-stone loose forward Tommy Crean and Andrew Clinch to the fore. The other major influence on the tour was prolific Moseley kicker John Byrne, who played in every game and kicked over 100 points.

Backs: Fullback: JF Byrne (Moseley and England) Centres and wings: CA Boyd (Dublin Univ), LQ Bulger (Dublin Univ and Ireland), OG Mackie (Cambridge Univ and Wakefield Trinity), LM Magee (Bective Rangers and Ireland), CO Robinson (Northumberland) Fly-halves and scrum-halves: SP Bell (Cambridge Univ), JT Magee (Bective Rangers and Ireland), MM Mullineux (Blackheath).

Forwards: WJ Carey (Oxford Univ), AD Clinch (Dublin Univ and Ireland), TJ Crean (Dublin Wanderers and Ireland), J Hammond (Cambridge Univ and Blackheath, capt), PF Hancock (Blackheath and England), R Johnston (Dublin Wanderers and Ireland), GW Lee*

(Rockliff), AWD Meares (Dublin Univ), W Mortimer (Cambridge Univ and Marlborough Nomads), RC Mullins (Oxford Univ), J Sealey (Dublin Univ and Ireland), AF Todd (Blackheath. (*replacement).
Manager: R Walker

— 'ER, I ONLY WANTED A SANDWICH . . .' —

Phil Bennett was stunned by the degree of interest the average New Zealander took in rugby. In his autobiography *Everywhere for Wales*, he said that on the 1977 tour he went into a café in the small town of Gisborne and waited to be served. When it came to his turn, the woman behind the counter looked at him and said: "Oh, your rucking's terrible. You want to go down to Otago and learn some rucking down there." Bennett, momentarily stunned, just looked at the woman and said: "But I only wanted a sandwich".

Will Carling tells a similar tale, of visiting a chemist on the 1993 tour to New Zealand trip and being served by a diminutive, white-haired lady. "Within seconds she was telling me she didn't think much of our backs," said Carling, "before launching into an analysis of where we were going wrong, which was as good as I have ever heard. The knowledge and interest over there is unbelievable."

— LIONS RECORDS: MOST TRIES ON A TOUR* —

Tries	Name	Venue	Games	Year
30	Randolph Aston	South Africa	19	1891
22	Tony O'Reilly	Australia, NZ and Canada	23	1959
22	Andrew Stoddart	Australia and New Zealand	27	1888
19	Peter Jackson	Australia, NZ and Canada	18	1959
19	Lawrence Bulger	South Africa	20	1896

*All official matches played in all countries including tests

— YOUNGEST OPPONENT —

The youngest test opponent ever faced by the Lions was Western Province wing Jack Hartley, who was just 18 years and 18 days old when he made his test debut against Bill Maclagan's 1891 Lions in the third test in Cape Town. That was, however, to be the youngster's only cap.

— LION-HEARTED IN KOREA —

Scottish lock Mike Campbell-Lamerton is best remembered as the stereotypical bumbling skipper of the 1966 Lions to New Zealand, the first party ever to lose all four tests. However, he was also a distinguished soldier who fought under Major General Douglas Kendrew, a former Lion, in both Korea and Cyprus, where he badly injured his back, hip and foot in a 60ft fall from a helicopter.

In Korea in May 1953, Campbell-Lamerton had already survived standing on an anti-personnel mine thanks to quick-thinking from one of his men and was one of two platoon commanders in the Duke of Wellington's regiment – the other was his lifelong friend, Scotland flanker David Gilbert-Smith – who were ordered to retake a hill called 'the Hook' from the Chinese. Such was the ferocity of the fighting as they did so that both men were recommended for the Military Cross, but in line with general military protocol it was decided that only one could be awarded. Campbell-Lamerton literally lost out on the toss of a coin, the MC going to Gilbert-Smith.

— THE GREATEST LIONS MATCHES: 2 —

South Africa 16, Lions 21
Third test
10th September 1938, Cape Town

Danie Craven's Springboks had returned from beating both the Wallabies and the All Blacks in 1937 to win the first two tests against Sam Walker's 1938 Lions. By the time of the final test against the injury-ravaged tourists they were in confident mood – too confident as it turned out.

In fact the South African players spent most of the week before the test arguing with their union about the quality of their hotel and threatening to strike if they weren't moved nearer to the town centre. The tourists, by contrast, threw caution to the wind and fielded the team suggested by Springbok selector Oubaas Markotter when asked by Walker. It was a team that included all eight of the Irishmen on tour and had four men playing out of position.

Although Llanelli wing Elvet Jones opened the scoring with a try, the makeshift side struggled badly in a first half of ferocious intensity at Newlands as South Africa, playing with the wind, replied with tries from Freddie Turner, Johnny Bester and Jan Lotz to lead 13–3 at half-time. It was a huge deficit and few would have given the Lions any chance of springing an upset.

Craven had been told the wind would die down at half-time, but instead it blew even harder, and with Irish forwards Walker, Blair Mayne and Bob Alexander to the fore, the Lions pack began to dominate. Gradually they fought their way back into the match, with hyperactive Bedford prop Gerald 'Beef' Dancer (who was never to be capped by his country) claiming the first try when he piled over after Walker and Mayne had combined off the back of a line-out. Then a penalty from Harry McKibbin was followed by Alexander's sixth and final try of the tour to take the lead by a point.

By now it was a thrillingly open game of tremendous cut and thrust, with South Africa retaking the lead through a penalty from Turner, only to see fullback Charlie Grieve kick the last ever four-point drop goal scored in South Africa (which would not have been given had the Springboks not sportingly signalled that it was good). Then, as the game reached its giddy climax, Scottish flanker Laurie Duff drove over to make it 21–16 to the Lions with just seconds to go.

There was, however, enough time for one last scrum. From that set-piece Craven broke on the blindside and fed Bester, whose pass put Welsh-speaking Springbok Dai Williams over in the corner – only for referee Nick Pretorius to call them back for a forward pass. Sam Walker may not have won the series but he was carried off in triumph as the Lions celebrated winning their first test in South Africa since 1910.

— COWARDLY LION —

The tack-sharp steelworker Bobby Windsor was either the instigator or the butt of more pranks than any Lion on the 1974 tour to South Africa. One night when the team was on safari in the Kruger National Park he climbed into bed with Tommy David, convinced that lions of the flesh-eating variety were out to get him. He convinced David too and the pair gripped each other in terror at the sound of roaring and banging on the walls of their hut – until Mike Burton, Chris Ralston and Ian McLauchlan piled in laughing.

— GREATEST LIONS XV: GAVIN HASTINGS (FULLBACK) —

Gavin Hastings

There is perhaps no match which better encapsulates what Gavin Hastings brought to the Lions than the game against the Maoris in 1993. The tour, of which he was captain, was in danger of going off the rails and the Maoris smelt a famous scalp. However, with the Lions trailing and looking listless Hastings' superhuman display almost single-handedly brought them back into the game to record a 24–20 win and deny the Maoris their first victory over the Lions.

Hastings always led from the front. Rock solid under the high ball, with pin-sharp kicking from hand, stoic defending and an ability to break into the line and pick up important tries, he is reckoned by many to be the best Scottish player of all time. He also proved himself to be an inspired leader in 1993 when he impressed the New Zealanders with his powerful running, balanced game and dogged determination.

Hastings was also a remarkably consistent goalkicker, kicking six penalties from six attempts in the first test in 1993 only for the Lions to lose 20–18 to the All Blacks thanks to a controversial late penalty. Hastings' prolific boot saw him top-score on consecutive Lions tours, collecting 66 points in 1989 and 101 in 1993. He still holds the record for the most points scored in Lions test matches with 66 and shares the record for the most penalties kicked in a test match with six.

Yet it was his ability to do something special that could change matches which marked him out. In 1989, in his first Lions tour, for instance, it was Hastings who scored the decisive try that won the second test and squared the series when he latched onto a bouncing pass from brother Scott, sold a dummy and handed off David Campese for the crucial try. Remarkably, he was concussed at the time and had to watch a television replay later to learn how he had scored.

Gavin Hastings' main competitors for the fullback berth in the Greatest Lions XV were (in order) JPR Williams, Andy Irvine, Lewis Jones, Ken Scotland, Tom Kiernan and Stewart Wilson.

Gavin Hastings stats
Born 3rd January 1962
Tours: 1989 & 1993
Tests: 1989 Aus 1, 2, 3; 1993 NZ 1, 2, 3
61 caps for Scotland 1986–1995
Clubs: Watsonians, Cambridge University, London Scottish

— THE ORIGINAL LION KING —

Barry John was not the first Welshman to be christened 'the King' by an adoring New Zealand public. Llanelli flanker Ivor Jones was such an impressive player on the 1930 tour that the sage of New Zealand rugby writing, Ron Palenski, says he was "for years regarded as the finest British player to be seen in New Zealand".

Jones had been chosen for the 1924 tour of South Africa, but had been unable to get enough time off work and had to withdraw, at which point he lost his place in the Wales side. Yet he was still one of the first players pencilled in when the 1930 tour party was chosen, and he didn't disappoint, not only setting up the winning try in the first test but filling in with some aplomb at scrum-half in the second test. He was also a handy kicker, drop kicking the first points of the tour against Wanganui, and then kicking ten penalties and two conversions in Australia. He went on to win 16 caps for Wales.

— THE LIONS ON TOUR: 1899 (AUSTRALIA) —

P21, W18, L3, Pts 333–90
Tests: L3–13 (Sydney), W11–0 (Brisbane), W11–10 (Sydney),
W13–0 (Sydney)

Organised and captained by London clergyman Rev Matthew Mullineux, the 1899 Lions were the first to be truly representative of all four home nations, with the 21-strong party containing two internationals each from England, Scotland and Ireland and one from Wales.

Mullineux had been to South Africa with the British tourists in 1896 but a return was out of the question because the Boer War broke out in 1899, so his became the first Lions party to tour just Australia, and the last until Finlay Calder's side 90 years later. After only three warm-up games Mullineux's men were comprehensively beaten in the first test to be played in Australia, before recovering to take the series 3–1. Nevertheless, it was a far more competitive series than the results might indicate and only Mullineux's decision to drop himself after the 13–3 first test thrashing saved the day.

The Blackheath fly-half was unique in that he was a Lions skipper who never played for his country, but when his place was taken by Durham's Charlie Adamson, who was to be the top scorer on the tour with 135 points, the results picked up almost immediately with the tourists winning 16 of the remaining 17 matches. Crucially, Adamson scored two tries and kicked four conversions and a penalty in the last three tests.

However, the star of the tour was Cardiff's threequarter Gwyn Nicholls, the first Welshman to win a Lions cap. The 'Prince of Threequarters' mesmerised teams the length and breadth of the country and ended the tour as top try-scorer with ten, as well as scoring a then Lions record of ten points in the fourth test.

Backs: Fullbacks: E Martelli (Dublin Univ), CEK Thompson (Lancashire) Centres and wings: AM Bucher (Edinburgh Acads and Scotland), GP Doran (Lansdowne and Ireland), EG Nicholls (Cardiff and Wales), ET Nicholson (Birkenhead Park), AB Timms (Edinburgh Univ and Scotland) Fly-halves and scrum-halves: CY Adamson (Durham), G Cookson (Manchester), MM Mullineux (Blackheath, capt).
Forwards: A Ayre-Smith (Guy's Hospital), FC Belson (Bath), GV Evers (Moseley), JS Francombe (Manchester), GR Gibson (Northern and

England), HGS Gray (Scottish Trialist), JW Jarman (Bristol), W Judkins (Coventry), TMW McGown (North of Ireland and Ireland), FM Stout (Gloucester and England), BI Swannell (Northampton). **Manager:** Rev MM Mullineux.

— CASH UP FRONT —

Each of the players who went on the 1930 tour of New Zealand had to advance a payment of £80 to cover "a dinner suit to be worn at evening meals on board ship" and to pay for spending money on tour. Many of the players from working-class clubs, especially those in Wales, couldn't afford it so their clubs stepped in to raise the money for them.

— DIRTY DEEDS —

The infamous '99 Call' (see *The 99 Call*, page 31) from the 1974 Lions was seen as an overreaction to the possibility that one of their number would be physically intimidated, but there have been plenty of examples before and since to suggest such fears were not completely fanciful.

The Lions have often found that their most influential player has been targeted and put out of the tour through foul play. In 1993, the Lions were dominating the line-outs when Andy Haden was drafted in to coach the All Blacks' jumpers ahead of the final test; during the deciding test the line-out was compressed and Bayfield was again tipped on the shoulder he damaged against Otago, a key moment in deciding the outcome of the series. The same thing happened in 2001 in Australia when Wallaby centre Nathan Grey late-tackled flanker Richard Hill, the player who made the Lions tick; again, it was an illegal play which put a key Lion out of the tour.

Most famously of all, though, in 2005 All Blacks captain Tana Umaga and Keven Mealamu spear-tackled Lions skipper Brian O'Driscoll in the opening moments of the first test, putting the distraught Irishman in hospital and ensuring he missed the rest of the tour.

— GREATEST LIONS XV: FRAN COTTON (LOOSEHEAD PROP) —

Fran Cotton

Prop Fran Cotton was a mighty man who took on the best in the world and destroyed them, even when playing out of position. The 6ft 2in, 17 stone Englishman is best known as the cornerstone of the 1974 Lions pack which humbled the mighty Springboks on their own patch, even though he had been asked to play in the unfamiliar position of tighthead prop.

However, he was arguably at his peak three years later when he toured New Zealand as a 30-year-old in 1977. Back in his accustomed position of loosehead, he was a mainstay of the Lions pack which outscrummaged the All Blacks so comprehensively that the New Zealanders took the unprecedented decision to opt for three-man scrums in the final test.

Cotton may have won seven caps on those two Lions tours, but if things had gone a little differently, he could have had up to 15 caps. After making his England debut in 1971 at the age of 23, he was unlucky not to travel with the 1971 Lions, although he was a reserve for the tour. And in 1980, he was the first choice loosehead and would have almost certainly have played in all four tests had he not suffered from an attack of viral pericarditis that required eight weeks of rest (it could have been worse: the initial diagnosis was of a heart attack).

Apart from his perfect scrummaging technique, innate physical strength and versatility, the pugnacious Cotton was blessed with a surprising turn of speed, good hands and a strong personality. A Lancastrian from Wigan (his father was a successful League player), Cotton's background as a PE teacher meant that he was formidably fit and in 1977 he took the forwards' training sessions. He was fast enough to captain England in the inaugural World Sevens tournament in 1973, while he was an outgoing character who often captained the Lions' midweek side in 1974 and 1977.

In fact, such was the regard in which he was held that the shrewd prop was asked to manage the 1997 tour to South Africa coached by his teammate from 1974 and 1977, Ian McGeechan. True to form, it was a tour characterised by innovative selections, expansive tactics and a hard-nosed approach that yielded an unexpected series win.

Cotton's main competitors for the greatest Lions loosehead prop position were (in order) Ian McLauchlan, Tom Smith, Hughie McLeod, David Sole and Syd Millar.

Fran Cotton stats
Born 3rd January 1947
Tours: 1974, 1977 & 1980
Tests: 1974 SA 1, 2, 3, 4; 1977 NZ 2, 3, 4
31 caps for England, 1971–81
Clubs: Coventry and Loughborough University

— SECRET CODE —

In 1971, Cardiff and Wales halfbacks Barry John and Gareth Edwards mystified the Kiwis – and many of their own side – by continuing their practice of discussing moves and tactics in Welsh. It certainly worked: the New Zealanders rarely laid a glove on 'the King'.

— THEY SAID IT 1 —

"I can well recall setting off for South Africa, not knowing what to expect. It quickly became obvious to me that South African rugby was superior to ours in many ways. They were more committed, they were fitter, they were better organised and they had a far greater pride and will to win than any team in these islands."
Willie John McBride on his first Lions tour in 1962.

"You guys from the British Isles believe in fairytales. There is no way with your haphazard approach and attitude that you will ever beat us."
Colin Meads to Willie John McBride.

"I think the third test could develop into open warfare. As far as I'm concerned the Lions have set the rules and set the standards and, if the officials are going to do nothing about it, then we are going to have to do it ourselves. We won't sit back and cop it again."
Wallaby skipper **Nick Farr-Jones** looks ahead to the deciding test in 1989 after an acrimonious and violent second test win for the Lions.

"You don't play Mickey Mouse rugby in the green and gold."
Former Wallaby skipper **Andrew Slack** damns David Campese for the stray third test pass that gifted Ieuan Evans the try which won the 1989 series.

"The Lions look like Pussycats."
Headline in the *Cape Town Argus* after the Lions first game of the 1997 series.

"If we don't destroy their composure we will be second. If we're not smarter than them we're buggered."
Graham Henry gives his pep talk before the first test in 2001.

— COOCH TO THE RESCUE —

During the 1993 Lions tour to New Zealand, Gareth 'Cooch' Chilcott single-handedly saved a man's life. The England prop was leading a group of rugby fans, who had gone white-water rafting for the afternoon, when their boat overturned after hitting a fallen tree trunk. One tourist, who could not swim, had his life vest ripped off him in the collision: Coochie held him afloat for 40 minutes with one hand while hanging onto an overhanging branch with the other before help finally arrived.

— OVERSEAS LIONS —

Players to have turned out for the Lions who were born and raised outside Britain or Ireland include: South African lock Cuthbert Mullins (1896), Kiwis Dr Pat McEvedy (1904 and 1908) and Arthur O'Brien (1904) who were medical students at Guy's Hospital; South African forward Brian Black (1930) who was the leading scorer in the series against the All Blacks; Aussie-born Scotland winger Ian Smith (1924); Canadian-born Scotland prop Grahame Budge (1950); Aussie legend Tom "Rusty" Richards (1910) who was in South Africa prospecting and qualified by dint of being a member of Bristol Rugby Club (See *The Wallaby Lion*, page 49); South African-born utility back Mike Catt (2001 and 2005); Aussie-born Wales lock Brent Cockbain (2005), and South Africa-born prop Matt Stevens (2005).

— LIONS RECORDS:
MOST TRIES IN A TEST MATCH —

For:

2	Alfred Bucher	v Australia (Sydney)	5th Aug 1899
2	Willie Llewellyn	v Australia (Sydney)	2nd Jul 1904
2	Carl Aarvold	v New Zealand (Christchurch)	5th Jul 1930
2	Jimmy Nelson	v Australia (Sydney)	26th Aug 1950
2	Malcolm Price	v Australia (Sydney)	13th Jun 1959
2	Malcolm Price	v New Zealand (Dunedin)	18th Jul 1959
2	Ken Jones	v Australia (Brisbane)	4th Jun 1966
2	Gerald Davies	v New Zealand (Christchurch)	10th Jul 1971
2	JJ Williams	v South Africa (Port Elizabeth)	14th Jul 1974
2	JJ Williams	v South Africa (Pretoria)	22nd Jun 1974

Against:

3	Tom van Vollenhoven	v South Africa (Cape Town)	20th Aug 1955
3	Stu Wilson	v New Zealand (Auckland)	16th Jul 1983
3	Frank Mitchinson	v New Zealand (Auckland)	25th Jul 1908

— BLAIR MAYNE: MAN OF ACTION —

All manner of men have worn the Lions jersey, but none, surely, have been rougher or tougher than Blair Mayne, the hulking second row whose rumbustious play during the 1938 tour of South Africa established him as one of the best forwards in the world. Mayne won three caps on that tour to go with the six he had won for Ireland, but the coming of war saw the end of his rugby career at just 24 years of age.

There were two sides to Mayne. One was the softly-spoken, poetry-loving Ulster lawyer, and the other was, in the words of fellow Lions tourist Harry Bowcott, "utterly fearless . . . our chief party animal". Welshman Bowcott was a famously tough man yet he saw no shame in ceding second place on that front to Mayne.

"He and old Bill Travers, the Welsh hooker who was a very tough boy too, would put on seamen's jerseys, go down the docks in Cape Town, wait until someone would say something rude about them and then demolish them!" chortled Bowcott. "That was their idea of a night out. Blair was the heavyweight champion of the Irish universities. Magnificent physique, and a very quiet fellow you thought wouldn't hurt a fly – until you saw him roused. Mad as a hatter."

Mayne was a famously hard-drinking carouser whose escapades are legendary. He once wrecked a hotel room with his bare hands in less than two minutes for a bet. Another time, he was dressed in white tie and tails and standing drinking at a bar in South Africa when a group of South African farmers invited him to accompany them to shoot some springbok. The excitable Mayne insisted they departed in the clothes they stood up in, returning at daybreak with an antelope across his shoulders and dripping blood all over his shirt. He then proceeded to tip the bloody beast into the bed next to his great pal, English wing Jimmy Unwin, who woke later to find himself with an unexpected bedfellow.

But it was in wartime expeditions with the SAS that Mayne found his true role in life. SAS founder David Stirling called him "a fighter of satanic ferocity"; the Germans thought far less kindly of him.

Stirling first met Mayne in prison, where he was languishing after flooring a senior officer, and the Scot immediately recognised a kindred spirit. He turned out to be a good judge of character: Mayne went on to win the DSO and three bars, the Croix de Guerre and Legion d'Honneur, making him the most decorated man in the SAS's history. When Stirling was captured, Mayne commanded the SAS with such success that at one stage 10,000 Germans were detailed to comb the desert for him.

Fellow soldiers talked of him "looking for some good killing" as he departed on various raids, most of which he approached with the same crazy tactic of steaming headlong through German lines in armoured vehicles with machine guns blazing. Mayne was always to the fore, his biggest tally for one day's work being the 12 Germans he gunned down when he single-handedly stormed an officer's mess, plus the 47 planes he also destroyed that day. His rage was so strong that when he ran out of fuses to blow up the final Messerschmitt, he ripped apart its cockpit with his bare hands.

But living an adrenaline-fuelled life for six years took its toll and despite the adoration of the people of his home town of Newtonards, he found readjusting to civilian life a daunting proposition. He died in a motor accident on 15th December 1955.

— MANDELA'S SUPPORT FOR LIONS —

He may be best known in rugby terms for his memorable cameo at the 1995 World Cup final at Ellis Park, but Nelson Mandela's favourite pre-Robben Island sporting memory is of standing in front of the advert for Quinn's bread at the same venue 40 years earlier, watching the 1955 Lions beat South Africa by a single point in front of 105,000 screaming fans when Springbok fullback Jack van der Schyff missed the last-gasp touchline conversion that would have seen the Boks win by a point (see *Greatest Lions Matches 3*, page 37).

Racial politics were already a feature of South African life by 1955 and the Lions team of that year found their hotel in Port Elizabeth picketed by the anti-apartheid 'Black Sash Women'. Many black South Africans, Mandela included, supported the Lions on that tour and lit newspaper bonfires whenever they won, as they did in 1974 when the Lions were beating the Springboks.

In his autobiography, *The Long Walk to Freedom*, published in 1994, Mandela wrote of the relish the prisoners on Robben Island took in the defeats of the Springboks and the guards' foul moods each time their national team lost.

If most of South Africa's white population were aghast, not all of their countrymen shared their dismay. "We had a slave mentality then," said Bantu Holomisa, a student in 1974 and a politician now. "We were taught that everything the Afrikaner did was perfect, but here was a team putting them in their place, humiliating them. The Lions were heroes to us."

— THE LIONS ON TOUR: 1903 (SOUTH AFRICA) —

P22, W11, L8, D3, Pts 231–138
Tests: D10–10 (Johannesburg), D0–0 (Kimberley), L0–8 (Cape Town)

By the early 1900s the 'Old Country' had little left to teach the colonials, yet it still came as a considerable surprise to Mark Morrison's tourists that playing standards in South Africa in 1903 were now a match for those of the Lions. Having lost just one out of 40 matches on their first two tours, the Lions side managed to win only half of their games in 1903. Even worse, after drawing the first two tests they lost the third test in Cape Town to a side packed with Western Province men and, with it, a series for the first time.

Morrison realised early on what was in store when the Lions lost the first three games of the tour in Western Province, and he would go on to lose to both Griqualand West and Transvaal twice, yet he was hamstrung by a desperate lack of quality backs. While the party included rugged forwards like Morrison himself, fellow Scots 'Darkie' Bedell-Sivright and Bob 'Bummer' Scott, Ireland captain Alf Tedford and England captain Frank Stout, only Newport threequarter Reg Skrimshire was a world-class back, and he had the bad luck to be faced with a Springbok back division that included all-time greats Paddy Carolin, Japie Krige and Bob Loubser.

In the end, the Lions' forwards failed to establish the dominance they expected, and while Skrimshire played in every game and was heroic in defence and attack, especially when scoring a virtuoso try in the first test, it wasn't enough to break the Boks. After two and a half tests of deadlock, the South Africans scored two second-half tries in the Cape Town mudbath that became known as the 'Umbrella Test' to win the match 8–0 and record their first series win in front of 6,000 spectators.

Backs: Fullback: EM Harrison (Guy's Hospital) Centres and wings: GF Collett (Gloucestershire), IG Davidson (North of Ireland and Ireland), AE Hind (Cambridge Univ), RT Skrimshire (Newport and Wales), EF Walker (Lennox) Fly-halves and scrum-halves: JI Gillespie (Edinburgh Accads and Scotland), LL Greig (United Services), PS Hancock (Richmond), RM Neill (Edinburgh Accies and Scotland).
Forwards: DR Bedell-Sivright (Cambridge Univ and Scotland), WT Cave (Cambridge Univ), TA Gibson (Cambridge Univ), JC Hosack (Edinburgh Wanderers), MC Morrison (Royal High School FP and Scotland, capt), WP Scott (West of Scotland and Scotland), RS Smyth

(Dublin Univ and Ireland), FM Stout (Richmond), A Tedford (Malone and Ireland), James Wallace (Wanderers), Joseph Wallace (Wanderers and Ireland).
Manager: J Hammond.

— LIONS RECORDS: MOST POINTS IN A TEST —

For:

31–0	v Australia (Brisbane)	4th Jun 1966
29–13	v Australia (Brisbane)	30th Jun 2001
28–9	v South Africa (Pretoria)	22nd Jun 1974
26–9	v South Africa (Port Elizabeth)	13th Jul 1974
25–16	v South Africa (Cape Town)	21st Jun 1997

Against:

18–48	v New Zealand (Wellington)	2nd Jul 2005
6–38	v New Zealand (Auckland)	16th Jul 1983
19–38	v New Zealand (Auckland)	9th Jul 2005
14–35	v Australia (Melbourne)	7th Jul 2001
16–35	v South Africa (Johannesburg)	5th Jul 1997

— SPIRITED RESPONSE —

During the 1971 tour of New Zealand a group of local evangelists would often be seen walking about with billboards asking the question, "What would you do if Jesus Christ came back to Earth?" The locals used to answer over a beer: "Put him on the wing and put Bryan Williams in the centre." But after Barry John had passed through town the word was, "The Lions have already got Him and He's playing fly-half."

— LIONS HITS THE RIGHT NOTE —

Before the 2005 Lions played Argentina at the Millennium Stadium, they were entertained by a performance from the London Welsh Male Voice Choir, which included 1971 skipper John Dawes.

— LIONS GREATEST XV:
KEITH WOOD (HOOKER) —

Keith Wood

Garryowen hooker Keith Wood was one of the most inspirational leaders of men in the modern game. Not only was he a fine hooker who was technically sound and one of the best front row ball-carriers of all time, but he also had an ability to energise all around him with his all-action style of play and forceful character.

He was beaten to the captaincy by Martin Johnson in 1997 and 2001 but was still one of the Lions' most influential players in both series. In fact, during the crucial second test in 1997 it was his break around the corner of a ruck and then his kick and chase that forced South Africa to concede a scrum in their own 22 and, indirectly, the score that won the game and the series for the Lions.

In Australia in 2001, from the moment he captained the Lions in the first game against Western Australia to the end of the third test, he was one of the standout players for the tourists. Indeed, he was so influential that later that year he was named as the IRB's inaugural World Player of the Year.

The sight of Wood's bald head in the thick of the action earned him the nickname of 'The Raging Potato' before the hyperactive hooker was later rechristened 'Uncle Fester' on the 2001 tour for his resemblance to the character in the *Addams Family*. Wood may have won many more caps were it not for his reckless disregard for his own safety, which was to mean several lengthy spells on the sidelines and a premature end to his career.

Wood's game was characterised by his fearless tackling and maniacal runs at the opposition defence. He holds the record for test tries by a hooker at 15, and scored four tries in the 1999 world cup against the USA. He is also the son of a Lion: prop Gordon Wood won two caps on the 1959 tour to New Zealand.

Wood's main competitors for the greatest Lions hooker position were (in order) Peter Wheeler, Bobby Windsor, Bryn Meredith, John Pullin, Brian Moore and Ronnie Dawson.

Keith Wood stats
Born 27th January 1972
Tours: 1997 & 2001
Tests: 1997 SA 1, 2, 3; Aus 1, 2, 3
58 caps for Ireland, 1994–2003
Clubs: Garryowen, Harlequins and Munster

— SPOORS ON THE DOORS —

Uncapped Englishman Jack Spoors remains the only player to score a try in each match of a Lions test series, the Bristolian wing scoring in all three tests in the 1910 series. Despite that feat, he was never capped for England, who preferred to select the Harlequins back division en masse. Only centre Jeff Butterfield in 1955 has equalled the feat of scoring in three tests on one tour, although he failed to score in the fourth and final test of that series against the Springboks.

— SPORTING ALL-ROUNDER —

A contender for the best all-round talent to have played for the Lions was the 1924 wing Stanley Harris, the former Blackheath record try-scorer who turned down the chance to be a part of the Great Britain Olympics squad in order to focus on his rugby.

After emerging as a schoolboy prodigy at Bedford Grammar School, he was wounded in World War I when a gunnery officer and took up ballroom dancing to relieve the boredom of convalescence: within a year he reached the finals of the World Ballroom Dancing Championships.

Although he won two Lions caps in 1920, he emigrated to South Africa soon afterwards, where he played for the famous Pirates club in Johannesburg.

Harris was a star of the 1924 series, heading the list of tour appearances with 15, and was rated as the pick of the Lions backs by the Springbok skipper Pierre Albertyn. Not only was he a hyperactive defender, but he was also an elusive runner whose try in the final test was rated the best of the series.

He remained in South Africa until the start of World War II, establishing a name for himself by winning Springbok colours at both boxing and tennis, winning the amateur light-heavyweight championship and representing South Africa in the Davis Cup. War changed his fortunes, but after surviving a spell on the Death Railway in Siam, Colonel Stanley Harris CBE played water polo for England and also won the mixed doubles at Wimbledon.

— LIONS RECORDS: BIGGEST TEST WINS AND DEFEATS —

Wins:

31–0	v Australia (Brisbane)	4th Jun 1966
24–3	v Australia (Sydney)	26th Aug 1950
24–3	v Australia (Sydney)	13th Jun 1959
28–9	v South Africa (Pretoria)	22nd Jun 1974
17–0	v Australia (Sydney)	2nd Jul 1904

Defeats:

6–38	v New Zealand (Auckland)	16th Jul 1983
18–48	v New Zealand (Wellington)	2nd Jul 2005
0–29	v New Zealand (Auckland)	25th Jul 1908

| 5–32 | v New Zealand (Dunedin) | 6th Jun 1908 |
| 14–35 | v Australia (Melbourne) | 7th Jul 2001 |

— KIT OF MANY COLOURS —

The Lions played the mighty Border province twice on their tour of South Africa in 1910. As the first match at East London was a charity match, the Lions players wore their club jerseys even though it was an official match.

— THE 99 CALL —

The theory of the infamous '99 Call' – a truncated version of the 999 emergency phone number – was that the 1974 Lions would never take a backward step, never allow one of their number to be targeted or intimidated, as had happened so often in the past. In practice, this meant that if there was any violence directed at a Lions player, the call would go out, at which point each of the Lions would stop playing and hit the man nearest to him on the basis that the referee couldn't send off the whole side.

The first time the use of the tactic became evident was four games into the tour when the Lions faced Eastern Province at Boet Erasmus stadium in Port Elizabeth. The story goes that before the game Springbok coach Johan Claasen went into the Eastern Province dressing room and incited the home pack to beat the Lions into the dust. They took him at his word, one forward head-butting Scotsman Gordon Brown (who had made his debut in the side which beat South Africa at Murrayfield in 1969) while he was on the floor, sparking a full-scale 30-man rammy. The Lions won 28–14 and proved they would not be intimidated.

The apogee of the '99 Call' came during the third test, after the Springboks had been reduced to shambling wrecks in the first and second tests. Facing a series loss, they brought out the biggest beasts in the country, spearheaded by the notorious Natal enforcer Johannes 'Moaner' van Heerden. The Springboks took the field 10 minutes late and, said Mervyn Davies, "with glazed eyes".

This test, which will forever be remembered as 'the Battle of Boet Erasmus', was probably the most violent in history. Just before half-time, van Heerden booted Lions hooker Bobby Windsor on the ground and it all kicked off. Brown had already thumped van Heerden so hard that he broke his thumb, but most people's memory of that match is JPR Williams running 50 yards from fullback to launch a withering salvo of punches at van Heerden, who cut and ran. For the remainder of the match fights broke out as the Lions refused to be cowed, all the while building up a match-winning lead that eventually saw them win 26–9.

John Reason described one particularly savage passage in his account of the tour, *The Unbeaten Lions*: "Windsor threw a punch in response to something that had happened on the ground, and in no time the fight escalated into a full '99' affair. Brown leapt in to hit Fourie and van Heerden and Kritzinger waded in and McBride went bobbing and weaving for what looked like 10 yards, throwing a succession of short lefts and rights while keeping his head prudently tucked in his shoulders, much after the style of Joe Frazier."

Some of those Lions, including Ian McLauchlan and Fergus Slattery, have insisted that the '99 Call' was a metaphor, that it was a state of mind rather than a concrete plan of action. To Welsh hooker Bobby Windsor, a 99 was a type of ice cream. "Can you imagine it?" he argued. "Some guy has slugged you or booted a colleague in the head and there you are shouting, '99'! First, you would never think to do so because you were piling in. Second, no one would hear you anyway."

— CLUB CORE —

Eight Newport players were named on the first official Lions tour in 1910, but that number from a single club has been matched once in modern history, when eight Leicester players toured New Zealand in 2005, albeit in a party nearly twice as big again as the 1910 squad. The Tigers picked for the Lions were: Neil Back, Martin Corry, Ben Kay, Lewis Moody, Geordan Murphy, Graham Rowntree, Ollie Smith and Julian White.

— THE LIONS ON TOUR: 1904
(AUSTRALIA & NEW ZEALAND) —

In Australia: P14, W14, Pts 265–51
In New Zealand: P5, W2, L2, D1, Pts 22–33
Tests: W17–0 (Sydney), W17–3 (Brisbane), W16–0 (Sydney); L3–9
(Wellington)

Lions teams at this stage were still by invitation only and were yet to represent the full playing strength of the four home unions. If the 1903 side which lost the series in South Africa had talented forwards and a lacklustre back division, exactly the opposite was true of the 1904 side.

The 1904 British tourists were led by fearsomely abrasive Scottish forward 'Darkie' Bedell-Sivright, the only survivor from the 1903 Lions, but it was the Welsh backs that sparkled. Had Gwyn Nicholls also toured, there would have been six Welsh backs on display, but as it was the magnificent Tommy Vile, Percy Bush, Rhys Gabe, Teddy Morgan and Willie Llewellyn played alongside two young London-based Kiwi medical students, Paddy McEvedy and Arthur O'Brien.

With two outstanding wing forwards in Blair Swannell and Boxer Harding the Lions lorded it around Australia, comfortably winning all 14 games including three tests in which the Wallabies scored just three points and conceded 50. Leading the rout was Percy Bush, the Cardiff fly-half making the same kind of impression on the Australians that Barry John was to make on the Kiwis 67 years later.

Things changed abruptly when they crossed the Tasman, however. The All Black 'Originals', featuring players like Billy Wallace, George Nicholson and 'Bronco' Seeling, had just beaten Australia 22–3 in Sydney and would cut a swathe through Britain the next year. New Zealand rugby was formidably strong and the Lions forwards struggled to cope with both the intensity of their New Zealand opponents and the 2-3-2 scrummage and rover Dave Gallaher. The Lions beat Canterbury by just a conversion, but at the cost of losing Bedell-Sivright with a broken leg, before beating Otago/Southland. But they lost 9–3 in the test, the first to be played in New Zealand, then had a scoreless draw against a Taranaki combination, finishing the second leg of their tour when they were eviscerated by Auckland.

Backs: Fullback: CF Stanger-Leathes (Northern) Centres and wings: JL Fisher (Yorkshire), RT Gabe (Cardiff and Wales), WF Jowett (Swansea and Wales), WM Llewellyn (Cardiff and Wales), PF

McEvedy (Guy's Hospital), ET Morgan (Guy's Hospital and Wales), AB O'Brien (Guy's Hospital) Fly-halves and scrum-halves: PF Bush (Cardiff), FC Hulme (Birkenhead Park and England), TH Vile (Newport).

Forwards: DR Bedell-Sivright (Cambridge Univ and Scotland, capt), TS Bevan (Swansea), SN Crowther (Lennox) DD Dobson (Oxford Univ and England), RW Edwards (Malone and Ireland), AF Harding (London Welsh and Wales), BF Massey (Yorkshire), CD Patterson (Malone), RJ Rogers (Bath), SM Saunders (Guy's Hospital), JT Sharland (Streatham), BI Swannell (Northampton), DH Trail (Guy's Hospital).

Manager: AB O'Brien.

— MCLAREN'S GREATEST XV —

Veteran television commentator Bill McLaren has watched the Lions play over many decades and is acknowledged as the 'voice of rugby'. This is his Dream Lions XV: **JPR Williams; Gerald Davies, Mike Gibson, Jeremy Guscott, David Duckham; Barry John, Gareth Edwards; Fran Cotton, Peter Wheeler, Graham Price, Willie John McBride (capt), Gordon Brown, Mike Teague, Fergus Slattery, Mervyn Davies.**

— ALL BLACK CROWD SEES RED —

The first test in Dunedin on 18th July 1959 saw the All Blacks leave the field with the boos of their compatriots ringing in their ears despite an 18–17 defeat of the Lions. Six penalties from Don Clarke's boot had beaten Irishman Ronnie Dawson's men, despite the free-flowing tourists playing some scintillating rugby and scoring four tries to their hosts' none.

As the teams trudged off the pitch the record crowd at Carisbrook chanted "Red! Red! Red!".

Indeed, although the All Blacks won that series 3–1, it was the Lions who scored nine tries to their hosts' seven – only Clarke's 27 penalties, often for obscure offences, kept the Kiwis' noses in front.

— GREATEST LIONS XV: GRAHAM PRICE (TIGHTHEAD PROP) —

Graham Price

Graham Price, who played in 12 consecutive tests for the Lions, is the touring team's most capped front-row forward and one of the most influential. Although neither the 1977 nor 1980 sides got their just rewards, they were both markedly superior to the All Blacks and Springboks in the scrum, and a lot of the credit for that must go to Price.

A member of Pontypool's fabled Viet Gwent, Price was rock solid as a scrummager and played in a formidable front row alongside Fran Cotton and hooker Peter Wheeler in New Zealand in 1977 when All Blacks skipper Ian Kirkpatrick decided to spare his crushed front five any further pain and opted for three-man scrums.

A quiet, thoughtful character who was born in Egypt and went to the same West Monmouth Grammar School that also turned out Lions legends Ken Jones and Bryn Meredith, the Welsh civil engineer announced his arrival on the international scene in 1975 when he scored a try for Wales on his debut. Although he was never conspicuous in the loose, especially towards the end of his career he became a useful ball-carrier. But it was for his strength, fearlessness and impeccable technique in the tight that he will be remembered.

Price's main competitors for the position of greatest Lions tighthead prop were (in order) Ray McLoughlin and converted loosehead Jason Leonard.

Graham Price stats
Born 24th November 1951
Tours: 1977, 1980 and 1983
Tests: 1977 NZ 1, 2, 3, 4; 1980 SA 1, 2, 3, 4; 1983 NZ 1, 2, 3, 4
41 caps for Wales 1975–83
Club: Pontypool.

— BILL'S ROADSIDE DASH —

Bill Beaumont was called up as a late replacement for Nigel Horton on the 1977 tour of New Zealand but got caught in a huge traffic jam on the M4. After an hour of waiting for the jam to clear, he realised that the only way he would make the plane and his first Lions tour would be if he were to run the remaining two miles along the hard shoulder in his blazer, carrying his bags on a searing hot day. He made it by the skin of his teeth, but found when he got to New Zealand to join the wettest, coldest tour of all time that some were questioning why he had bothered. "If I were you, Bill, I'd flick off home on the next plane," said Irishman Willie Duggan when Beaumont met him at the airport in Auckland.

— FAMILY TIES —

Llanelli and Lions back-rower Derek Quinnell, father of Llanelli and Lions back-rower Scott Quinnell, is also the brother-in-law of Lions legend Barry John, whose sister Medora is Quinnell's wife.

— THE GREATEST LIONS MATCHES: 3 —

South Africa 22, Lions 23
First test
6th August 1955, Johannesburg

The Lions' victory over the Springboks in front of 105,000 spectators at Ellis Park in 1955 is widely recognised as the greatest match involving the touring side, and came at the beginning of a series which remains the most entertaining in which the Lions have ever been involved.

This epic confrontation had it all: two sides determined to play running rugby, nine tries, a lead that changed hands four times, courage in the face of adversity as the Lions played the whole second half with 14 men, and a result that was in doubt until the very last kick of the game. It was so exciting that one spectator fell down dead of a heart attack in the second half.

Led onto the park by dirt-trackers second row Ernie Michie in full highland dress and playing his bagpipes, Robin Thompson's Lions were the quickest out of the blocks when Jeff Butterfield made a sublime break and drew fullback Jack van der Schyff before putting wing Cecil Pedlow in for the first try. South Africa replied with two outstanding penalties from van der Schyff and then moved 11–3 in front when skipper Stephen Fry put wing Theunis Briers in after a break by diminutive scrum-half Tommy Gentles. Shortly before half-time, Cliff Morgan's guile allowed Butterfield to make it 11–8 at the interval.

Although flanker Reg Higgins was stretchered off with torn knee ligaments shortly into the second half, the Lions were still on the front foot thanks to a searing break and try from Morgan. When van der Schyff was twice deceived by the bounce of the ball, leading to tries for Tony O'Reilly and Jim Greenwood, the Lions led 23–11 having stunned the Ellis Park crowd with 15 points in ten minutes.

Yet the loss of a forward and playing at altitude took its toll, and the Springboks roared back with tries from Josias Swart, prop Chris Koch and Briers, the third coming just seconds from time. All of which left van der Schyff with a conversion from halfway between the posts and touchline for the win. O'Reilly couldn't bear to look, and later quipped that he was instead in direct communication with the Vatican. If so, it worked, as the kick flew wide of the upright to give the Lions a famous victory.

The picture of van Schyff's despair as his kick passed the posts is one of the most famous images in Springbok rugby; the fullback never played for South Africa again, emigrating to Rhodesia to become a crocodile hunter.

— THE LIONS ON TOUR: 1908
(NEW ZEALAND & AUSTRALIA) —

In Australia: P9, W7, L2, Pts 127–48
In NZ: P17, W9, L7, D1, Pts 184–153
Tests: L5–32 (Dunedin), D3–3 (Wellington), L0–29 (Auckland)

One of the main motivations of Boxer Harding's 1908 Anglo-Welsh tour was to halt the spread of Rugby League, which the 1905 Originals had encountered in the north of England and which Kiwi George Smith had already implanted in Sydney. As manager George Harnett said, "If New Zealand is not to be abandoned to professionalism, the visit of a British team is a necessity."

However, the Irish and Scots, still smarting from their belief that the 1905 All Blacks tour was a professional venture refused to send any players. Although New Zealand skipper John Stead reckoned that the tourists were as talented as their hosts, they lacked the fitness, intensity or backs to compete with the Kiwis. It didn't help that they also made the most of all the host country had to offer. One report spoke of "extravagance, tarradiddles and a crawling unquietness" adding that some players "were unwisely wooed to folly by the damsels of Dunedin".

Whether or not this was true, the Lions were also lightweight behind the scrum and no match for the top teams, losing to Wellington, Otago, Canterbury, Taranaki and Auckland before being obliterated in the first and third tests. Only in the second test, where the New Zealand selectors fielded a second team in a blizzard, were the Lions competitive, holding the All Blacks to a 3–3 draw.

They fared better across the Tasman Sea, beating all bar Western Districts and New South Wales, demonstrating the gulf in class between the game in New Zealand and that in Britain and Australia.

Backs: Fullbacks: JCM Dyke (Coventry and Wales), EJ Jackett (Falmouth and England) Centres and wings: FE Chapman (Hartlepool Rovers), RA Gibbs (Cardiff and Wales), RB Griffiths (Newport), JP 'Ponty' Jones (Pontypool and Wales), JP 'Tuan' Jones (Guy's Hospital), PF McEvedy (Guy's Hospital), HH Vassall (Oxford Univ and England), JL Williams (Cardiff and Wales) Fly-halves and scrum-halves: J Davey (Redruth and England), H Laxon (Cambridge Univ), WL Morgan (London Welsh), GL Williams (Liverpool).
Forwards: HA Archer (Guy's Hospital), R Dibble (Bridgewater Albion and England), PJ Down (Bristol), RK Green (Neath), AF Harding

(London Welsh and Wales, capt), GR Hind (Guy's Hospital), FS Jackson (Leicester), GV Kyrke (Marlborough Nomads), E Morgan (Swansea), WL Oldham (Coventry and England), JAS Ritson (Northern), TW Smith (Leicester), LS Thomson (Penarth), JF Williams (London Welsh and Wales).

Manager: GH Harnett.

— DISMAL DEBUTS —

After the Lions had destroyed the Springboks during the first test in South Africa in 1974 in one of the most one-sided test matches Newlands has ever staged, Dr Danie Craven, the autocratic greybeard who dominated South African rugby, could barely contain his wrath. His ire eventually oveflowed at the post-match banquet in the Ostrich Hall when it came to presenting the six caps who made their debuts in that day's test match with their Springboks blazers.

"It hurts me to be giving you these because you have not earned them," was his opening line. "I have to present a cap and a blazer to [wing] Chris Pope, who created a record by becoming the first Springbok ever to play for his country without touching the ball." Then he moved on to Peter Whipp, the centre: "At least he did better than Pope. He touched the ball once." Next it was the turn of giant second row Kevin de Klerk, who "looks a big man here, but wasn't a big man on the field", and then finally on to flanker Boland Coetzee, "he is the old man of the team, and he played like one". Ouch.

— LION-SIZED FAN ARMY —

Lions supporters following tours in large numbers started in earnest in New Zealand in 1993, when just over 300 people followed the Lions on licensed supporters tours. By the time the 2001 Lions hit Australia, that number had swelled to 10,000 on official tours and an estimated 10,000 on DIY tours, plus all the ex-pats and travellers already in Australia. In 2005, a vast travelling army numbering 29,000 (according to official NZ government figures) invaded New Zealand and the organisers of the 2009 tour are estimating that approximately 55,000 travelling fans will cheer on the Lions in South Africa.

— SING-ALONG WITH THE LIONS —

The 1977 tourists may not have been able to win tests, but with a record 18 Welshmen in the party they could certainly sing. Just to prove it, they decided to cut a record, with all the proceeds going to the Queen's Silver Jubilee Trust Fund. With Gordon Brown as the choirmaster, a studio was set up in the Waitangi Hotel. The cover versions on the *Sing-along with the Lions* album were as follows:

Lion Blue
You Are My Sunshine
Take Me Home Country Roads
Wild Mountain Thyme
Island of Dreams
House of the Rising Sun
Rose of Tralee
Summer Holiday
Flower of Scotland
Where Have All the Flowers Gone
There's a Goldmine in the Sky
The Lord is My Shepherd
Amazing Grace
The Canoe Song
Banks of the Ohio
Moonlight Bay
For Me and My Girl
Abie My Boy
Wait Til The Sun Shines Nellie
I Don't Want to Go Home
Bye Bye Blackbird
Show Me the Way to Go Home.

— RED OR WHITE, SIR? —

No compensation for loss of earnings ('broken-time payments') was ever contemplated before the game went professional in 1995, but on the 1904 and 1908 tours players were paid three shillings a day 'wine money'.

— GREATEST LIONS XV: MARTIN JOHNSON (SECOND ROW) —

Martin Johnson

The only man to captain the Lions on two tours, Englishman Martin Johnson is a colossus. His finest hour was captaining the 1997 Lions to a series victory in South Africa, and it is fitting that he remains the only man other than Willie John McBride to have led a Lions team to a series victory against the Springboks in the 20th Century.

Johnson's career was inextricably linked with the Lions. Although he had won a single cap for England in the 1993 Five Nations against France having been called in as a last-minute replacement for Wade Dooley, he was first catapulted into the public consciousness when he was called out as a replacement for the 1993 Lions after Dooley flew home following his father's death. Johnson performed so impressively that he was immediately drafted into the test team for the second test and also played in the third (although he can only remember so much of the deciding test after he was accidentally concussed by a wild haymaker from teammate Martin Bayfield).

By the time of the 1997 Lions, Johnson was an imposing figure who led from the front. At 6ft 7in and almost 19 stone, Johnson was a big beast, but it was his mental toughness and ruthless edge, honed as a young player when he spent two years in New Zealand, that really set him apart. In South Africa he was one of the most consistent ball-winners in a pack that constantly looked as if it would be overwhelmed.

In Australia in 2001, Johnson was again a central player on the tour, especially in the decision to play an expansive game as the Lions took the Wallabies apart during the first test. However, Johnson's Lions career ended on a low when, pushing for the winning try in the final minutes of the third test against the Wallabies in 2001, he called a lineout on the Australian line to himself, only to see Justin Harrison rise and claim the ball, allowing the Wallabies to stymie the final attack and clear their lines.

Johnson's career has been one of non-stop achievement. Not only did he play for New Zealand Colts, but he also captained England to a World Cup win in 2003 and led Leicester to back-to-back Heineken Cup wins.

Martin Johnson wins a place as the front jumping second row of the Greatest Lions XV ahead of (in order) Gordon Brown, Paul Ackford, Bill Beaumont, Delme Thomas and Rhys Williams.

Martin Johnson stats
Born: 9th March 1970
Tours: 1993, 1997 & 2001
Tests: 1993 NZ 2, 3; 1997 SA 1, 2, 3; Aus 2001 1, 2, 3
84 caps for England, 1993–2003
Club: Leicester

— LIONS PLAY AUSSIE RULES —

Not only did the 1888 tourists play 35 matches of rugby union (the 22-strong party lost just two and drew six) on their 11-month, 54-match tour of Australia and New Zealand, but while in Victoria they also played 19 games of what later became Australian Rules Football. These were exhibition games to make money (there was virtually no rugby union played in Victoria) to fund the tour, but despite never having played the code the party picked up the rules very quickly and, amazingly, won nine of their 19 matches.

— HOW MANY ARE YOU? —

After the 1974 Lions won the third test to assure themselves of victory in the series, they held a monumental wrecker of a party in their Port Elizabeth hotel. With furniture disintegrating, a succession of fire extinguishers set off and the hotel lobby under several inches of water, the hotel manager stormed off to find Willie John McBride. It wasn't difficult as McBride had removed the door and doorframe to his room several days earlier when the night porter refused to give him the key when he arrived back in the early hours.

"Mr McBride," screamed the manager, "your players are wrecking my hotel."

"Are there many dead?" asked McBride, sitting cross-legged on his bed dressed in nothing but his y-fronts and puffing on his pipe.

"I want every one of you locked up. The police are on their way."

"And tell me," puffed McBride with a beatific smile as the demolition of the hotel continued in the background, "these police of yours – will there be many of them?"

— AUBREY'S CAMEO ROLE —

Stentorian Englishman Charles Aubrey Smith, who went on to become the most famous English actor in 1930s Hollywood, starring in *The Prisoner of Zenda* and *The Four Feathers*, was one of three cricketers already in Australia who joined Shrewsbury and Shaw's original 1888 touring party when it was in Australia and appeared for the side when they played Victorian Football (now Aussie Rules) in Melbourne.

The 6ft 4in Englishman's first love was actually cricket, which he had played for Cambridge University and Sussex (he was on WG Grace's side in the Player v Gentlemen match at Lord's) before he left to play cricket in Australia in 1887. After his stint Down Under playing cricket and rugby, he travelled to Johannesburg, where he planned to become a gold prospector. While there, the round-the-wicket bowler captained England against South Africa on his only test appearance before heading to Hollywood in 1929. Once installed in California, he became an actor and set up the Hollywood Cricket Club whose members also included Boris Karloff, David Niven, Clark Gable, Douglas Fairbanks Jnr, Laurence Olivier and PG Wodehouse. Aubrey Smith was knighted for his services to Anglo-American relations in 1944.

— THE LIONS ON TOUR: 1910 (SOUTH AFRICA) —

P24, W13, L8, D3, Pts 290–236
Tests: L10–14 (Johannesburg), W8–3 (Port Elizabeth), L5–21 (Cape Town)

After the travails of 1903 and 1908, where British teams had failed to win any of six tests against the South Africans or New Zealanders, the first official tour supported by all four home unions was labouring under few illusions about the strength of opposition they would meet. This tour was an especially daunting prospect given that Paul Roos's legendary Springboks, who toured the British Isles in 1906, had beaten Wales and Ireland, drawn with England and lost only to Scotland (Watsonian forward Louis Speirs played that day and was in the 1910 touring party but didn't play in any of the three tests).

The tourists, led by mercurial and popular Irishman Tom Smyth, were right to be cautious and found the going was even tougher than when Mark Morrison's men toured there in 1903. A punishing schedule, a lack of seasoned internationals – only 14 capped players were in the original party and Newport provided seven of the squad – and a merciless attrition rate on the injury front further handicapped the tourists, who, while losing just six of their 21 non-test games, lost the test series 2–1.

The series is remembered most vividly for the emergence of the young English phenomenon 'Cherry' Pillman, the young Blackheath flanker who dominated the series. Pillman's absence from the first test through injury proved decisive. In a hard-fought game which was poised at 11–10 with just minutes to go, the home side's best player, Duggie Morkel, made a break from his own line and released CHL 'Cocky' Hahn with an intelligent kick ahead to the left which the back seized upon and raced away to score the winning try.

The second test was a remarkable game in which Pillman, who played at fly-half in a side ravaged by injuries, put in a match-winning performance that is still reckoned one of the best solo displays ever seen in South Africa. It wasn't enough though: in the third test, an early injury to Welsh fullback Stanley Williams saw the tourists play most of the game with only 14 men. They were in touch but exhausted at half-time, and were overrun after the interval as the Springboks outscored them by four tries to one and went on to win by the enormous margin of 21–5.

Backs: Fullback: SH Williams (Newport) Centres and wings: AM Baker (Newport and Wales), AR Foster (Derry and Ireland), JP Jones (Pontypool, Newport and Wales), ME Neale (Bristol), RCS Plummer (Newport), JA Spoors (Bristol), CG Timms (Edinburgh Univ), KB Wood (Leicester) Halfbacks: NF Humphreys (Tynedale), GAM Isherwood (Cheshire, Sale, Old Alleynians), AN McClinton (North of Ireland and Ireland), E Milroy* (Watsonians and Scotland).

Forwards: WJ Ashby (Queen's Coll, Cork), EO Crean (Liverpool), FG Handford* (Kersal and England), H Jarman (Newport and Wales), CH Pillman (Blackheath and England), OJS Piper (Cork Constitution and Ireland), J Reid-Kerr (Greenock Wands and Scotland), TJ Richards* (Bristol), Dr WA Robertson (Edinburgh U and Hartlepool Rovers), DF Smith (Richmond and England), Dr T Smyth (Newport and Ireland, capt), LM Speirs (Watsonians and Scotland), R Stevenson (St Andrews Univ and Scotland), W Tyrrell (Queen's Univ Belfast and Ireland), PD Waller (Newport and Wales), J Webb* (Abertillery and Wales).

(* replacements).

Managers: W Cail and Walter E Rees.

— RECORD VICTORIES —

The biggest margin of victory recorded by any Lions team came on the 2001 tour of Australia when they beat Western Australia 116–10 in Perth, with Dan Luger and Scott Quinnell scoring three tries each in a record Lions haul of 18.

The biggest win in New Zealand was recorded in 2005, when Brian O'Driscoll's men beat Manawatu 109–6 in Palmerston North, with Welsh wing Shane Williams scoring five of the 17 tries scored by the Lions that day. The biggest win in South Africa remains the 97–0 defeat of South Western Districts at Mossel in 1974, a match in which JJ Williams scored a record six tries.

— ROCKING LIONS —

There is an American rock group called the British Lions, whose most recent album, *Trouble With Women*, was released in 2002.

— LIONS RECORDS:
MOST POINTS IN A TEST MATCH —

For:

18	Jonny Wilkinson	v Australia (Sydney)	14th Jul 2001
18	Gavin Hastings	v New Zealand (Christchurch)	12th Jun 1993
18	Tony Ward	v South Africa (Cape Town)	31st May 1980
17	Tom Kiernan	v South Africa (Pretoria)	8th Jun 1968
16	Lewis Jones	v Australia (Brisbane)	19th Aug 1950

Against:

33	Dan Carter	v New Zealand (Wellington)	2nd Jul 2005
25	Matt Burke	v Australia (Melbourne)	7th Jul 2001
19	Matt Burke	v Australia (Sydney)	14th Jul 2001
18	Don Clarke	v New Zealand (Dunedin)	18th Jul 1959
18	Allan Hewson	v New Zealand (Auckland)	16th Jul 1983

Note: Didier Camberabero scored 19 points for France in a game against the 'British Lions' on 4th October 1989 in Paris, during a match to celebrate the French Revolution which was never ratified as a proper Lions encounter.

TOURING MATCH —

Tries	Final score	Opponent	Date
18	116–10	v Western Australia	8th Jun 2001
17	109–6	v Manawatu	28th Jun 2005
16	71–3	v Western Australia	22nd Sep 1930
16	70–6	v Eastern Canada	29th Sep 1959
16	97–0	v South West Districts	29th May 1974

— LANE IN PAIN —

Stuart Lane holds the most unenviable record in Lions history, the shortest career. The Cardiff and Wales wing was stretchered off with damaged knee ligaments within 50 seconds of the start of the 1980 tour opener against Eastern Province in Port Elizabeth. The damage was so severe that he was flown home from South Africa and never played for the Lions again.

— GREATEST LIONS XV: WILLIE JOHN MCBRIDE (SECOND ROW, CAPTAIN) —

Willie John McBride

With a record-equalling five tours, a record 17 caps and the captaincy of the first team of the 20th Century to win a series in South Africa, Willie John McBride stands head and shoulders above the contenders for the position of greatest Lion of all time. He remains the greatest leader of the Lions.

McBride only came to rugby as a 17-year-old, but because he had been working on the family farm since his father died when he was five, he had a physicality way beyond his teenage years.

He first toured with the Lions as a 21-year-old, having played just four games for Ireland. He was to learn about Lions rugby the hard way, touring South Africa and New Zealand three times with parties that had gifted backs but were physically dominated up front by their more hard-nosed hosts. That apprenticeship – which entailed being on the losing side in his first nine Lions tests – was to form the basis for the triumphs of 1971 and 1974.

By 1971, he had already been playing international rugby for ten seasons and some suggested that he was over the hill. Yet McBride was made pack leader and was determined to physically confront the Kiwis so that his pack would provide enough ball for his talented backs. In that he was spectacularly successful, comfortably outplaying the best forward of all time, Colin Meads, as the Lions won their first ever series in New Zealand.

If 1971 was good, 1974 was the high water mark of Lions rugby. It was McBride and coach Syd Millar, his fellow Lions, Ireland and Ballymena forward, who agreed to physically confront the Springboks. From his tours in 1962 and 1968, McBride knew that they had to destroy the South Africans up front and unravel the aura of Springbok invincibility. That they did so, with a few of McBride's '99 Calls' sparking some epic brawls, owed much to the Ulsterman.

Off the pitch, McBride was a laconic, easy-going man of much charm. When it came to rugby, however, he had a mental intensity and hard edge that marked him out as one in a million, and the greatest Lion of them all.

McBride gains entry to the Greatest Lions XV as a middle-jumping second row ahead of (in order) the English trio of Wade Dooley, Martin Bayfield and Maurice Colclough.

Willie John McBride stats
Born: 6th June 1940
Tours: 1962, 1966, 1968, 1971, 1974
Tests: 1962 SA 3, 4; 1966 NZ 2, 3, 4; 1968 SA 1, 2, 3, 4; 1971, NZ 1, 2, 3, 4; 1974 SA 1, 2, 3, 4
63 caps for Ireland, 1962–75
Club: Ballymena.

— WILD FOR THE LIONS —

Groupies are nothing new, as this account of the 1955 Lions, who apparently found the ladies' attention "tougher to handle than playing rugby" shows.

"Britain's touring team have become the pin-up boys of South Africa," wrote journalist Margaret Lessing. "Schoolgirl bobby-soxers and women fans are mobbing them wherever they go. Red-headed 19-year-old (Tony) O'Reilly is pin-up number one, and then comes Johnny Williams, one of 12 players who may settle here, captain Robin Thompson, Jeff Butterfield, Cliff Morgan and Cecil Pedlow."

— THE WALLABY LION —

The legendary Tom 'Rusty' Richards is one of only two players who have turned out for both the Wallabies and the Lions.

The son of a Queensland gold miner, Richards saw rugby as his way out of poverty – especially after his brother Bill played for Queensland against New South Wales – and set about making himself into a top player. Running miles each day, building up his abdominal muscles by getting a younger brother to punch them relentlessly and honing his reactions by catching chickens, he developed into the ultimate wing forward.

Richards had spent a couple of years prospecting in South Africa in 1905, but although he was a standout for Transvaal in the Currie Cup, he was ruled ineligible for a Springbok cap because he hadn't been in the country long enough. Fed up, he went to Europe, turning out for Biarritz before playing for Bristol in England and turning out for the Gloucestershire team that played the Springboks in 1906.

When he scored the first try for Australia against Wales on the Wallabies' first overseas tour in 1908/09, *the Times* wrote, "If ever the earth had to select a rugby team to play Mars, Tom Richards would be the first player to be selected." When the Australians beat Cornwall to win gold in the 1908 Olympic final, Richards was the dominant player and scored a try.

He returned to South Africa in 1910 and was asked to play for that year's injury-struck Lions (he qualified as a member of the Bristol club) and he went on to play in two of the three tests and nine of the last 11 matches on tour.

Richards didn't stay in the Transvaal long, and soon returned to Australia. After captaining Sydney club Manly he toured North America with the Wallabies in 1912 before enlisting as soon as war broke out. There he was to distinguish himself once again, being one of the first Anzac troops onto the beach at Gallipoli and then winning the MC for "conspicuous gallantry and devotion to duty" by leading the group of soldiers which broke the Hindenburg line at Bullecourt. Unfortunately, he was gassed in France and died at the age of 52 in Brisbane. But his memory lives on: the Lions and Wallabies now contest the Tom Richards Cup.

— THE LIONS ON TOUR: 1924 (SOUTH AFRICA) —

P21, W9, D3, L9, Pts: 175–155
Tests: L3–7 (Durban), L17–0 (Johannesburg), D3–3 (Port Elizabeth),
L16–9 (Cape Town)

This was the year when the Empire struck back. The 1924 tour was a disaster, with Ronald Cove-Smith's side coming perilously close to a whitewash in the tests and at one stage going eight games without a win. South African rugby was just entering a golden era and British rugby was in a slump, and the result was something of a mismatch.

The first major problem for the tourists was that they were not remotely representative of the strength of British rugby. Although Wavell Wakefield was missing, they were still highly competitive up front, where legends such as Jammie Clinch and the England duo of Cove-Smith and Tom Voyce were the nucleus of a battle-hardened pack which didn't take a step backwards on tour

Behind the scrum, however, they were disastrously weak. There was some talent in Rowe Harding, Stanley Harris, Ian Smith and Herbert Waddell, but the unavailability of several key players – only two of the much vaunted Scottish back division were available – meant that too many mediocre players got a look-in.

When a chronic run of injuries made matters worse, the tourists were terribly exposed: both Voyce and Clinch were forced to start matches in the backs, while two of the three fullbacks were injured so that non-kicking Dan Drysdale was landed with the goal-kicking duties with catastrophic results, his missed penalty from in front of the posts in the drawn third test summing up the tour.

"Many unkind things were said about our wining and dining, but that was not the explanation of our failures," wrote Swansea wing Rowe Harding, one of the few successes in the Lions back division. "The long train journeys (often of 48 hours' duration) and hard grounds took a heavy toll. The British pack was a very fine one and was hardly ever worsted, but behind the scrums we hardly ever rose above mediocrity.

"The real reason for our failure was that we were not good enough to go abroad as the representatives of the playing strength of these islands. It is not sufficient to send abroad some players of international standard and others who are only second class. Every member of the team must be absolutely first class or disaster is bound to overtake it."

Backs: Fullbacks: D Drysdale (Heriot's FP and Scotland), WF Gaisford (St Bart's Hospital), TW Holliday (Aspatria and England) Centres and wings: JH Bordass (Cambridge Univ), WR Harding (Swansea and Wales), SW Harris (Blackheath and Blackheath), RM Kinnear (Heriot's FP), RB Maxwell (Birkenhead Park), IS Smith (Oxford Univ and Scotland), W Wallace (Percy Park) Fly-halves and scrum-halves: WA Cunningham* (Lansdowne and Ireland), HJ Davies* (Newport and Wales), VM Griffiths (Newport and Wales), H Waddell (Glasgow Accads and Scotland), H Whitley (Northern), AT Young (Blackheath and England).

Forwards: AF Blakiston (Blackheath and England), MJ Bradley (Dolphin and Ireland), TN Brand (North of Ireland), JD Clinch (Dublin Univ and Ireland), Dr R Cove-Smith (Old Merchant Taylors and England, capt), DS Davies (Hawick and Scotland), RG Henderson (Northern, Durham Univ and England), KGP Hendrie (Edinburgh Univ, Heriot's FP and Scotland), RA Howie (Edinburgh Univ, Kirkcaldy and Scotland), NC MacPherson (Newport and Scotland), D Marsden-Jones (Cardiff, London Welsh and Wales), J McVicker (Belfast Collegians and Ireland), Dr WJ Roche (UC Cork, Newport and Ireland), A Ross (Kilmarnock and Scotland), AT Voyce (Gloucester and England).

(* replacement)

Manager: H Packer.

— LIONS' RECIPE FOR CURRIE CUP —

South Africa's Currie Cup competition was kick-started by Bill Maclagan's 1891 Lions, who were given a golden cup by the head of the Union-Castle Shipping Line, Sir Donald Currie, with the express instruction to award it to the best team they faced on the tour. That turned out to be Griqualand West, who pushed the Lions all the way on a rock-hard pitch in their first game, a try from Maclagan and a penalty from Alan Rotherham accounting for the 3–0 win. So the Griquas became the first holders of the Currie Cup, which they subsequently presented to the South African Rugby Board to be played for in subsequent years as the premier domestic trophy, the inaugural tournament being won by Western Province in 1892.

— RAY'S IN A RIGHT OLD JAM —

Pontypool steel worker Ray Prosser had rarely been out of Wales, so the 1955 Lions tour was a bit of an eye-opener. In particular he struggled with the eloquence of the Harlequins lock and City banker David Marques who, despite having a Welsh mother, had a cut-glass English accent. "There 'e goes again, always using long bloomin' words like 'marmalade'," said Prosser of the Englishman.

— LIONS RECORDS: BIGGEST WINS AND DEFEATS IN TOURING MATCHES —

Wins:

116–10	v Western Australia	8th Jun 2001
109–6	v Manawatu	28th Jun 2005
97–0	v South West Districts	29th May 1974
83–6	v Queensland President's XV	12th Jun 2001
71–3	v Western Australia	22nd Sep 1930

Defeats:

10–38	v Waikato	29th Jun 1993
3–28	v New South Wales	10th Sep 1930
0–20	v Eastern Province	16th Jul 1955
8–27	v Transvaal	2nd Jul 1910
0–19	v Cape Colony	27th Jul 1910

— KNOW WHAT AMIN? —

Ugandan despot Idi Amin was not only a keen swimmer and once bet the equivalent of £1m that none of his countrymen could beat him at breaststroke but was also his country's light-heavyweight boxing champion. Less well known is the fact that he was a keen rugby player who was on the bench when the Lions beat an East African XV 39–12 in Nairobi in the final match of the 1955 tour.

— WISH YOU WERE HERE —

In New Zealand in 1977 it rained and rained and rained. Peter Wheeler sent a postcard home saying: "It only rained twice last week – once for three days, the other time for four."

— GREATEST LIONS XV:
FERGUS SLATTERY (OPENSIDE) —

Fergus Slattery

Quicksilver Irish breakaway Fergus Slattery remains the prototype of the perfect openside flanker. With incredible speed off the mark, shrewd game sense, tenacious tackling and an ability to recycle ball from the breakdown before the heavy brigade had arrived, Slattery was one of the stars of the all-conquering 1974 team.

Despite being just 22 when he toured New Zealand with the 1971 Lions, Slattery made such an impact that he is still revered in the Land of the Long White Cloud. However, after being picked ahead of John Taylor for the third test the Dublin auctioneer woke up with a rasping cough and selflesslessly pulled out. He also missed out on the fourth test after Taylor had a stormer in the third.

In 1974, though, he was peerless. Willie John McBride's pack dismantled the Springboks up front, and behind the scrum Slattery's ability to glide across the hard grounds of the Veldt stopped South African attacks at source, delaying the Bok halfbacks and centres for long enough to allow the Lions' big men to hove to.

With his incredible speed, good upper body strength, willingness to put himself in harm's way and superhuman fitness, Slattery was the perfect link man. He even eclipsed that Springbok legend, flanker Jan Ellis.

He was, however, denied the chance to apply the real coup de grace in the final test in 1974 when, with the score tied at 13–13 and the Lions leading the series 3–0, he was denied a try by referee Max Baise, who claimed he had already blown the whistle by the time the Lions openside forced his way over the Springbok line.

Slattery wins his place as the openside in the Greatest Lions XV at the expense of (in order) Richard Hill, Bill McKay, Finlay Calder, Terry Cobner, John Taylor, Peter Winterbottom and Rodger Arneil.

Fergus Slattery stats
Born: 12th January 1949
Tours: 1971 and 1974
Tests: SA 1, 2, 3, 4
61 caps for Ireland, 1970–84
Club: Blackrock College

— METAL MAN —

Wales and Pontypridd fly-half Neil Jenkins played the whole of the 1997 tour of South Africa with a six-inch metal plate and eight screws in the arm that he broke playing against England on 15th March that year. The whole thing had to be removed when he got home.

— FIRST TEST —

The first Lions test match took place on Thursday 30th July 1891 when Bill Maclagan's tourists beat South Africa by one goal and one try to nil in Port Elizabeth. Over 6,000 spectators turned out to watch the match.

— THE LIONS ON TOUR: 1930
(NEW ZEALAND & AUSTRALIA) —

In New Zealand: P21, W15, L6, Pts 420–205
In Australia: P7, W5, L2, Pts 204–113
Tests: W6–3 (Dunedin), L10–13 (Christchurch), L10–15 (Auckland),
L8–22 (Wellington); L5–6 (Sydney)

The 1930 tour was the first of the modern era, and the first where the team was officially known as 'Lions'. It was the first long 28-match tour and the first tour to New Zealand to be played with the four test format. It also had a huge impact on the way the game was played in New Zealand.

The Kiwis had developed several variations in the way the laws were applied and this tour addressed that issue. The most contentious was the system of a 2-3-2 scrum allied to playing a wing forward, which Lions manager Bim Baxter denounced as "cheating" after a game against Taranaki. In 1931, he ensured that the International Rugby Board banned the practice as well as several others then common in New Zealand, but his forthright views during the tour didn't endear him to his hosts.

On the pitch, the Lions were handicapped by the absence of stars such as England captain Wavell Wakefield and Irish wing George Stephenson. Simply getting a tour party togther proved difficult – over 100 players were invited before the organisers assembled the party of 29. Injuries played their part too, with the loss of scrum-half Wilf Sobey in the first game a crushing blow. The inability of skipper Doug Prentice to command a place on merit was also problematic, as was the 'them and us' feeling fostered by the autocratic Baxter.

Yet the Lions boasted quicksilver backs and were still fearsome opponents. Welsh fullback Jack Bassett was highly rated, as was imperious Englishman Carl Aarvold, who scored two magnificent tries in the second test and another in the Third. His centre partner Harry Bowcott was a teak-tough Welshman, while English fly-half Roger Spong was the stand-out back. Up front, Irish strongman George Beamish and Welsh flanker Ivor Jones – nicknamed 'the King' and rated the best British forward to visit New Zealand before the war – provided genuine class.

The Lions won 15 of 21 games in New Zealand, losing only to Wellington, Canterbury and Auckland, and won the first test when Jones broke in the dying moments to put wing Jack Morley in for the winning try. They could not sustain that level of play, however, and Cliff Porter's All Blacks came back to win the remaining three tests, with the second and third being very tight affairs. The Lions were also beaten by New South Wales and Australia on the way home.

Backs: Fullbacks: J Bassett (Penarth and Wales), WGM Bonner (Bradford) Centres and wings: CD Aarvold (Cambridge Univ, Blackheath and England), HM Bowcott (Cambridge Univ, Cardiff and Wales), R Jennings (Redruth), TE Jones-Davies (London Welsh and Wales), JC Morley (Newport and Wales), PF Murray (Wanderers and Ireland), AL Novis (Blackheath, Army and England), JSR Reeve (Harlequins and England) Halfbacks: TC Knowles (Birkenhead Park), H Poole (Cardiff), WH Sobey (Old Millhillians and England), RS Spong (Old Millhillians and England).

Forwards: GR Beamish (Leicester, RAF and Ireland), BH Black (Oxford Univ, Blackheath and England), MJ Dunne (Lansdowne and Ireland), JL Farrell (Bective Rangers and Ireland), JM Hodgson (Northern), HCS Jones (Manchester), I Jones (Llanelli and Wales), DA Kendrew (Woodford, Leicester, Army and England), SA Martindale (Kendal and England), HO O'Neill (Queen's Univ, Belfast and Ireland), D Parker (Swansea and Wales), FD Prentice (Leicester and England, capt), H Rew (Blackheath, Army and England), WB Welsh (Hawick and Scotland), H Wilkinson (Halifax and England).
Manager: J Baxter.

— A NICE DROP —

The only player ever to score two drop goals for the Lions in a test match was Phil Bennett who twice fired the ball between the uprights against South Africa in Port Elizabeth on 13th July 1974. No team has ever scored more than one drop goal against the Lions in a test match.

— RED ALL OVER —

In 2001 there were so many red-shirted Lions supporters in Australia that before the second test in Melbourne ARU chairman John O'Neill arranged for yellow scarves and bin bags to be distributed around the stadium so it would look more like a home game.

— LIONS NICKNAMES —

'Noddy' – Fran Cotton
'Uncle Fester' – Keith Wood
'The Abbot' – Hughie McLeod
'The Bear' – Iain Milne
'Buzz Lightyear' – Jeremy Davidson
'Bowleglio' – Lawrence Dallaglio
'Great White Shark' – John Jeffrey
'The King – Ivor' Jones/Barry John
'Merv the Swerve' – Mervyn Davies
'Broon Frae Troon' – Gordon Brown
'Shaggy' – Will Greenwood/Shane Hogan
'Flipper' – Tony Ward
'Commanchero' – Jim Renwick
'Toony' – Gregor Townsend
'Teapot' – Peter Wright
'Del Boy' – Damian Cronin
'Archie' – Paul Burnell
'Mighty Mouse' – Ian McLauchlan
'Axel' – Anthony Foley
'Ginger Monster' – Neil Jenkins
'Donkey' – Chris Oti
'Alfie' – Gareth Thomas
'Nugget' – Martyn Williams
'Wellies' – Stephen Jones
'Melon' – Gethin Jenkins
'Squeaky' – Rob Andrew
'Billy Whizz' – Jason Robinson
'Judith' – Craig Chalmers
'BOD' – Brian O'Driscoll
'Rodge' – Ronan O'Gara
'Strawman' – Peter Winterbottom
'Pitbull' – Brian Moore

There are also some nicknames that are no longer as acceptable as they maybe once were. The Welsh centre 'Pussy' Jones comes into this category, as do 1903 Lions skipper 'Darkie' Bedell-Sivright (so called for his swarthy complexion) and 'Bummer' Scott, the tough Glaswegian forward who was one of the standout players in 1903. The Springboks have had their share of non-PC nicknames, including 1896 Springbok skipper 'Fairy' Heatlie.

— LAST UNCAPPED LION —

The last uncapped player to tour with the Lions was 24-year-old Harlequins centre Will Greenwood, who was selected to tour South Africa in 1997 with Martin Johnson's Lions before he had played for England.

Greenwood didn't win a test cap with the Lions on that tour, but did go on to play in two tests in 2005 (he would also probably have played in 2001 but for injury), go on three Lions tours and amass 55 caps for England.

Given the many opportunities for fringe players to win caps, it seems highly unlikely that any uncapped players will tour with the Lions in future.

— GOLDEN GIFT —

The Lions in 1891 were presented with 'commemorative' gold medals when they played two matches in the diamond-mining centre of Kimberley, home to the biggest man-made hole on Earth.

— GOING GREEN —

The first time South Africa ever wore the myrtle green shirts they wear today was during the last test against the Lions in 1896. Seeking to avoid a 4–0 whitewash in their white shirts having lost the first three tests, skipper-for-the-day Barrie 'Fairy' Heatlie decided a break with tradition was needed and the only alternative kit to hand was that of the defunct old boys' club of his school, Diocesan College ('Bishops') in Cape Town.

Playing in the unfamiliar green, South Africa won the test 5–0, to scenes of enormous jubilation, but the shirt wasn't there to stay. During the Lions' next visit in 1903, the Springboks wore white jerseys in the drawn first and second tests. However, the custom at the time was that the Springbok skipper was nominated by the host province, so when Western Province hosted the third test and Heatlie was again named skipper of a side containing 11 Western Province men, he once again chose to play in myrtle. The Springboks won 8–0 and they never changed back to white. At this stage the collar was still white, and white remains South Africa's change strip.

— THE GREATEST LIONS MATCHES: 4 —

New Zealand 6, Lions 9
Fourth test
19th September 1959, Auckland

Like the 1950 and 1955 Lions, the 1959 tourists were defined by fleet-footed backs and rugged forwards, who together played an expansive attack-at-all-costs brand of running rugby. They had been unlucky to lose the first and second tests, in which they were arguably the better side but were undone by All Black fullback Don Clarke's prodigious goal kicking and some baffling refereeing, but finally gained some measure of vindication by becoming the first and so far only Lions side ever to win the final test against the All Blacks.

The turnaround was even more staggering given their collapse in the third test, but for the fourth test the pack was stuffed full of Irishmen – six in all – who added some real steel to the forward exchanges, none more so than flanker Noel Murphy and lock Bill Mulcahy.

It was the backs, however, who had been the star attractions throughout a highly popular tour and who drew 60,000 to Eden Park that September afternoon. They didn't disappoint, with the three stars of the show scoring beautiful tries that brought the crowd to their feet.

First up was wing Peter Jackson, who beat three defenders and crossed after Tony O'Reilly had made a break and delivered an ostentatious one-handed pass. Then, shortly after half-time, came O'Reilly himself, claiming another of his record 22 tries on that tour after scrum-half Andy Mulligan broke down the blindside. Finally, fly-half Bev Risman scorched in from 40 yards after an audacious reverse pass from Mulligan wrong-footed the whole All Black defence.

It was fitting that three backs should score the tries that won the game, but even then the shadow of Clarke's boot lay heavy. The fullback scored two penalties but, unusually, missed a relatively easy chance which would have given New Zealand an undeserved draw. It says much for the regard in which the Lions were held that the crowd greeted the final whistle with screams of "Red! Red! Red!", just as they had done after the first test.

As Fred Boshier wrote in Wellington's *Evening Post*, the result "gave the Lions the consolation which everyone felt they richly deserved . . . the British forwards not only held the All Black pack . . . but frequently played over it."

— THE LIONS ON TOUR: 1938 (SOUTH AFRICA) —

P23, W17, L6, Pts 407–272
Tests: L12–26 (Johannesburg), L3–19 (Port Elizabeth), W21–16 (Cape Town)

Ulsterman Sam Walker's 1938 tour to South Africa pitted the free-running Lions against the undisputed world champions. Benny Osler's Springboks had whitewashed the four home unions in 1931/32, and Danie Craven's side won a 2–1 series victory in New Zealand in 1937, where they were rated as the best side ever to visit that country, and had beaten the Wallabies 2–0 on the way home. Faced with a side that included Springbok legends like Craven, Boy Louw and Gerry Brand, expectations of the Lions were low.

Those expectations weren't helped by the absence of key potential Lions such as Wilson Shaw, Wilf Wooler, Willie Davis, Charles Dick, Fred Huskison, George Horsburgh and Cliff Jones, yet the Lions proved to be popular, entertaining and highly competitive visitors. Swashbuckling Welshmen Haydn Tanner and Vivian Jenkins, English fly-half Jeff Reynolds, and centres Harry McKibbin and Bill Clement were prominent performers in the backs. Up front, rumbustious Irish lock Blair Mayne was a stand-out, as were Welsh hooker Bunny Travers and two breakaways, Scot Laurie Duff and Irish cricket cap Bob Alexander, a rugged player who was destined not to see out the war.

The Lions were bedevilled by injuries, particularly behind the scrum where they played a different scrum-half in each test, while only McKibbin played all three tests. Their reaction was to throw caution to the wind, scoring more points than any previous visitors to South Africa, Not only did it win games – their only provincial losses were to Western Province (twice) and Transvaal – it won them many friends.

The Lions even managed to claim their first test win in South Africa since 1910 when they won the third test 21–16 after being 13–3 down at half-time, but it was for their carefree play that they are remembered. Craven reckoned that the Springboks' performance in the first test was the best he ever saw, and it needed to be as the Lions led three times in the first half.

The second test, played in 96° heat and immediately dubbed the 'Tropical Test', was memorable only for a Vivian Jenkins penalty from 10 yards inside his own half as the Lions were well beaten. The final test of one of the greatest series' ever played was a classic, as a Lions team containing eight Irishmen snatched the most dramatic victory imaginable (see *The Lions' Greatest Matches 2*, page 14).

Backs: Fullbacks: CF Grieve (Oxford Univ and Scotland), VGJ Jenkins (London Welsh and Wales) Centres and wings: CV Boyle (Dublin Univ and Ireland), WH Clement (Llanelli and Wales), EL Jones (Llanelli), R Leyland, (Waterloo and England), DJ Macrae (St Andrews Univ), HR McKibbin (Queen's Univ, Belfast and Ireland), BE Nicholson (Old Whitgiftians, Harlequins and England), EJ Unwin (Rosslyn Park and England) Halfbacks: GE Cromey (Queen's Univ, Belfast and Ireland), JL Giles (Coventry and England), GJ Morgan (Clontarf and Ireland), FJ Reynolds (Old Cranleighans, Army and England), H Tanner (Swansea and Wales).

Forwards: R Alexander (North of Ireland and Ireland), SR Couchman (Old Cranleighans), GT Dancer (Bedford), PL Duff (Glasgow Acads and Scotland), CRA Graves (Dublin Wands and Ireland), WG Howard (Old Birkonians), RB Mayne (Queen's Univ and Ireland), ME Morgan (Swansea and Wales), AG Purchas (Coventry), AR Taylor (Cross Keys and Wales), WH Travers (Newport and Wales), S Walker (Belfast Instonians and Ireland, capt), JA Waters (Selkirk and Scotland), I Williams (Cardiff).

Managers: Col BC Hartley, HA Haigh-Smith (assistant).

— WARTIME HEROES —

The 1938 Lions party was packed with men who went on to win medals in World War II. Both Welsh wing Bill Clement and Scottish centre Duncan Macrae were awarded Military Crosses during the conflict, Clement for his actions in the Battle of the Bulge and Macrae for his heroism under fire in France as a medic.

In 1941, two of the three men leading the Allied retreat from Crete were rugby men. The overall commander of allied forces on the island was a Kiwi, General Bernard Freyberg, and his aide-de-camp was former All Blacks skipper Jack Griffiths, who went on to win the Military Cross. Conducting the air defence of the island was Lions legend, and later air marshal, George Beamish.

— THEY SAID IT 2 —

"Get your retaliation in first."
After the 1966 Lions forwards were roughed up at every opportunity, 1971 Lions coach **Carwyn James** demands that his Lions get on the front foot in New Zealand.

"Somewhere along the line it becomes a mental thing. We grew in confidence; we came to believe it was possible to beat the All Blacks."
Gerald Davies on the 1971 tour.

"There will be no Carisbrook next Saturday."
The week after 'the Battle of Canterbury', the NZRFU issue a statement calling for restraint after All Blacks coach Ivan Vodanovich says that if the Lions lie over the ball the scene will resemble Paschendale.

"If you've got a bloke from round the corner refereeing he will always be biased because he has to go back and live round the corner."
Willie John McBride on the vexed question of neutral referees.

"Now go out and show the world what all of Stradey knows."
Llanelli coach **Carwyn James's** last words to Scarlets fly-half Phil Bennett before the first test against South Africa in 1974.

"Take no prisoners."
1974 skipper **Willie John McBride**'s famous words before the tour to South Africa.

"You know you're up against it when the ref shouts 'our ball!' at the put-in."
McBride on South African referees.

"Remember lads, there's no retreat. No more talk now. Just make peace with yourselves."
McBride before the first test in South Africa in 1974.

"There was a belief that we had the players to beat these guys. If one set didn't function then we should bring in another. We never believed until years later that the Lions were that good."
1974 Springbok skipper **Hannes Marais**.

"We had a pack to take on the world, in fact we had two packs that could, and did, lick the All Blacks and by the final test New Zealand were reduced to pitiful three-men scrums. I have never seen opposition forwards so humbled in the tight. But I took my eye off the backs, didn't show them the attention to detail I should have."
1977 Lions coach **John Dawes**.

"This match will go down in history as Dave Loveridge's test. I believe that was one of the finest exhibitions of halfback play in the history of test rugby."
Bryce Rope, All Blacks coach, after the second test in 1983.

"We have kidded ourselves for 12 years. In 1971 the Lions beat the All Blacks and we thought we had conquered the world. I said after the Scotland tour here two years ago that All Black rugby was more physical and aggressive. It is time we stopped kidding ourselves about the standard of rugby in the Five Nations. You could not have a more dedicated, committed team than these Lions, but they were not good enough – they were like Lions to the slaughter. I have failed."
1983 Lions coach **Jim Telfer**.

"At the end of the tour, there were two distinct parties. There was a tour party that was playing test matches and trying to win a test series and there were guys who had jumped off the train, who just didn't front up. That's why I believe New Zealand is the hardest place to go on tour because you have to front up there every week and when you're down in the pissing wet rain of Invercargill on the Tuesday night before one of the test matches and you're going to get your head kicked in, you've just got to be prepared to take it. I think there were probably three or four guys who just weren't prepared and weren't hard enough and prepared to work hard enough."
Gavin Hastings on the 1993 tour in *High Balls and Happy Hours*.

— COMING FROM BEHIND —

The only British sides ever to win a series after losing the opening test are those of 1899 and 1989, the first two tours to visit just Australia.

— GREATEST LIONS XV: MERVYN DAVIES (No8) —

Mervyn Davies

Along with Fergus Slattery and Roger Uttley, Welshman Mervyn Davies formed the best Lions back row of all time. In the opinion of many commentators and players, Merv the Swerve was not only the best No8 ever to play for the Lions, but simply the greatest of No8s, full-stop.

Davies was an immense presence in both the 1971 and 1974 tours, and remains a legendary figure in both New Zealand and South Africa. A tall and surprisingly slight figure, Davies nevertheless had a rare raw-boned strength, a remarkable standing jump that allowed him to dominate the back of the lineout and, above all, an uncanny sense of timing and anticipation.

Those qualities were to stand him in good stead in New Zealand, where he was a constant source of lineout ball (Colin Meads said that Davies "had us donkey-whipped" at the back of the lineout), while the almost telepathic understanding he had developed with scrum-half Gareth Edwards was a key factor in the Lions' series win. A deft handler, and distributor of genuine quality, he was not just a playmaker but also a perceptive defender and tireless tackler.

Just how tireless was obvious on the 1974 tour to South Africa. The party had departed with talented Englishman Andy Ripley in pole position to wear the No8 jersey, but Davies' inspired play in matches such as the ones against Orange Free State and Northern Transvaal got him into the Test side, and one scything tackle on Springbok flanker Jan Ellis in the mud at Cape Town, plus a rampaging drive that set up Edwards for the winning drop-goal, confirmed that he would stay there for the remaining three tests.

Such was the regard in which Davies was held that he was to be offered the captaincy of the 1977 Lions. With his Lions experience and what he had learned as he led a Wales side in transition to a Grand Slam in 1976, he would have been the perfect choice. Unfortunately aged 29 he suffered a career-ending brain haemorrhage during a Welsh Cup semi-final in 1976, with only prompt medical attention at the sidelines saving his life.

Mervyn Davies was selected for the Greatest Lions XV ahead of (in order) Dean Richards, Jim Telfer, Iain Paxton, Jim Greenwood and Willie Duggan.

Mervyn Davies stats
Born 9th December 1946
Tours: 1971 & 1974
Tests: 1971 NZ 1, 2, 3, 4; 1974 SA 1, 2, 3, 4
38 caps for Wales, 1969–76
Clubs: London Welsh and Swansea

— LIONS RECORDS: MOST POINTS ON A TOUR* —

Pts	Name	Venue	Games	Year
188	Barry John	Australia and New Zealand	17	1971
156	Andy Irvine	South Africa and Rhodesia	14+1	1974
136	Charlie Adamson	Australia	20	1899
133	Phil Bennett	New Zealand and Fiji	16	1977
127	Fred Byrne	South Africa	21	1896
124	Ollie Campbell	New Zealand	11	1983

*All official matches played in all countries including tests

— CRICKETING LIONS —

Arthur Shrewsbury, one of the two entrepreneurs who managed a highly successful cricket tour to Australia in 1884/85 and put together the first Lions tour, was one of the foremost cricketers of his day and the first test cricketer to score 1,000 runs. He was such an effective opening batsman for Nottinghamshire that WG Grace's constant refrain when asked whom he would like to open the batting for England was, "Get me Arthur!"

Shrewsbury's partner was Alfred Shaw, with whom he had arranged several cricket tours. Along with cricketer Andrew Stoddart, the men conceived the idea of a rugby tour to the southern outposts of the Empire (all three were in Australia but got an agent, Mr Turner, to recruit players on their behalf). Shrewsbury had been WG Grace's predecessor as the main opening batsman for the England cricket team, and when Grace moved aside it was Stoddart, who captained England when they played Australia in Sydney in February 1888, who stepped in to succeed him. Stoddart also went on to captain the 1894/95 England cricket side which retained the Ashes, his impressive innings of 173 in the second test in Melbourne being the turning point of the series.

— IN THE RING WITH ROCKY —

Many Lions were also decent boxers, including Scottish Amateur Heavyweight champion 'Darkie' Bedell-Sivright, Stanley Harris and Rob Wainwright, but the best of them all was Welsh centre Jack Matthews, the Cardiff doctor whose destructive tackling on the 1950 tour to New Zealand earned him the nickname 'Iron Man'.

Just 5ft 8in but weighing 14 stone, the hugely powerful player was a young medical student during the war when he stepped into the ring with a young Italian-American serving in the American Army in Wales. After three punishing rounds at the St Athan airbase in 1943, there was nothing to choose between Matthews and Rocco Marchegiano – who was soon to change his name to Rocky Marciano – and the contest was declared a draw.

"That's just the way it was, boxing for the fun of it," Matthews later told journalist Peter Jackson. "There were no knock-downs and I was still there at the end of three rounds. I didn't know who I'd fought until years later [but] I'd been told before the fight that he was a useful boy who could punch a bit. He was a hard boy alright."

— FIT FOR DUTY —

Wales fly-half Bleddyn Williams was the outstanding threequarter of his generation and a master of the sidestep, but despite dominating midfield play until his retirement in 1955, he almost missed the 1950 tour. After injuring a knee in the Wales trial in January 1950 he spent three months in plaster, missing Wales' first Grand Slam since 1911, but was still selected to tour with the Lions provided he could prove his fitness.

This he did when playing for Cardiff against Bath just ten days after he came out of plaster. Still not match fit, his inside centre was 19-year-old Cliff Morgan, who reminded him as they ran onto the field that "the best way to prove you're fit is to score in the last minute". Williams idled through the game, and with three minutes to go Morgan wandered over and said: "Are you ready?" "I said 'as ready as I'll ever be'," remembers Williams. "He got the ball from the scrum on the halfway line, waltzed past the flanker on the other side, beat the other flanker, came up to the fullback and I was able to get outside him and I scored a try under the crossbar."

Despite having 'proved' his fitness, Williams was still not genuinely match fit by the time of the first test in Dundein, but went on to captain the Lions in the remaining three tests in New Zealand and the test in Australia, establishing a reputation as one of the best players ever to visit the Land of the Long White Cloud. He reinforced that standing in 1953 when he captained both Wales and Cardiff to wins over the touring All Blacks.

— A GOOD DAY'S WORK —

When Tony O'Reilly was involved in a car crash in Dublin shortly before winning his final cap at the age of 35, he was in hospital when a nurse asked whether he earned more than the £11,000 threshold for free treatment. "Some days I do, some days I don't," replied the business magnate.

— NOSE MATTER —

Ulsterman Bill McKay earned plaudits during World War II as a commando of great daring, and the Lions flanker demonstrated how tough he was in 1950 when he broke his nose in the second test and then played in the third test.

— THE LIONS ON TOUR: 1950
(NEW ZEALAND & AUSTRALIA) —

In New Zealand: P23, W17, L5, D1, Pts 420–162
In Australia: P6, W5, L1, Pts 150–52
Tests: D9–9 (Dunedin); L8–0 (Christchurch); L6–3 (Wellington);
L8–11 (Auckland); W19–6 (Brisbane); W24–3 (Sydney)

Few tours have been so good-natured or such a shot in the arm for the game as the 1950 Lions. The Lions may have failed to win any of the tests in New Zealand – although they drew one and won both tests in Australia – but they established a reputation as a skilled and talented side that loved to play a running game. That was, however, partly because the Lions struggled to match the intensity of New Zealand's forward play.

The 1950 tour was the first in which every top international, with the exception of Wales skipper John Gwilliam and English powerhouse lock John Matthews, was available. The 30-strong party that left for New Zealand was dominated by 13 of the Welsh Grand Slam team of 1950, and also contained nine of the Ireland team which won back-to-back championships in 1948 and 1949, five Scots and three Englishmen.

Captained by Ireland hooker Karl Mullen, the backs were the undoubted stars. Brightest among them were legendary Irish outside-half Jack Kyle and Welsh sprinter Ken Jones, with Welsh centres Jack Matthews and Bleddyn Williams also outstanding. Up front, Irish flanker Bill McKay, Welsh lock Roy John and his compatriot, blindside Bob Evans, were the pick of the forwards.

The Lions had arrived in good heart as the All Blacks had lost six tests in a row, four in South Africa in 1949 and two in Australia, where they had sent a second team. However, when Otago beat the Lions 23–9 and showed how vulnerable the tourists were to strong-rucking sides, their fate was sealed.

The Lions still almost won the first test against the over-confident All Blacks, with only a late try from home skipper Ron Elvidge saving the draw after tries from Jones and Kyle and an unexpectedly strong showing from the Lions pack. The loss of McKay early in the second test hampered the Lions, and in the third only a try by Elvidge, after he had dislocated his shoulder, earned the All Blacks a three-point victory. The final test is remembered for ferocious rucking, with Pat Crowley again leading the way, and a stunning length-of-the-field try from Ken Jones which began when 20-year-old replacement Lewis Jones, who was an unexpected star of the tour, broke out from under his own posts before passing to his countryman deep into All Black territory for an easy finish.

Backs: Fullbacks: WB Cleaver (Cardiff and Wales), B Lewis Jones* (Devonport Services, Llanelli and Wales), GW Norton (Bective Rangers and Ireland) Centres and wings: NJ Henderson (Queen's Univ, Belfast and Ireland), KJ Jones (Newport and Wales), MF Lane (UC Cork and Ireland), J Matthews (Cardiff and Wales), R Macdonald (Edinburgh Univ and Scotland), DWC Smith (London Scottish and Scotland), MC Thomas (Devonport Services, Newport and Wales), BL Williams (Cardiff and Wales) Halfbacks: AW Black (Edinburgh Univ and Scotland), JW Kyle (Queen's Univ, Belfast and Ireland), I Preece (Coventry and England), G Rimmer (Waterloo and England), WR Willis (Cardiff and Wales).

Forwards: GM Budge (Edinburgh Wanderers and Scotland), T Clifford (Young Munster and Ireland), C Davies (Cardiff and Wales), DM Davies (Somerset Police and Wales), RT Evans (Newport and Wales), DJ Hayward (Newbridge and Wales), ER John (Neath and Wales), PW Kininmonth (Oxford Univ, Richmond and Scotland), JS McCarthy (Dolphin and Ireland), JW McKay (Queen's Univ, Belfast and Ireland), Dr KD Mullen (Old Belvedere and Ireland, capt), JE Nelson (Malone and Ireland), VG Roberts (Penryn and England), JD Robins (Birkenhead Park and England), JRG Stephens (Neath and Wales). (* replacement)

Managers: Surgeon-Captain LB Osborne (RN), EL Savage (assistant)

— TOO BUSY TO PLAY BEN HUR —

If glamorous Irish Tony O'Reilly had been less of a blushing violet, Charlton Heston may never have got to play *Ben Hur* or picked up an Oscar for Best Actor.

O'Reilly had been keen on amateur dramatics as a schoolboy and at university, and with American director William Wyler scouring the world for a lead for his new epic, a friend of O'Reilly's submitted his name. Despite several offers of an audition, O'Reilly refused on the basis that, "I was in the middle of my law studies and they had to come first".

— TRAGIC TOUR —

The 1888 tour was surrounded by tragedy. First of all the hugely popular original captain Bob Seddon drown in the Hunter River near Maitland when sculling (his boat flipped over and he couldn't free himself from the bindings). His talented successor Andrew Stoddart was to commit suicide in 1915, as had the tour's promoter Arthur Shrewsbury, who shot himself in 1902, wrongly believing he had an incurable illness.

The Kiwis were not immune to tragedy either. The skipper of the New Zealand national side (they were then called the Natives, and played in dark blue with a gold fern), drop kick specialist Joe Warbrick, who remains, at 15, the youngest player to have played first-class rugby in New Zealand, was one of three people who died when the Waimungu geyser in Rotorua exploded unexpectedly in 1903. He was the organiser and captain of the 1888/89 Natives side which toured Britain, playing 107 games. (The side also included four of his brothers.)

— OFF THE BEATEN TRACK —

The Lions have occasionally strayed from their four main destinations of South Africa, New Zealand, Australia and Argentina.

In 1908, for example, they stopped off for an unofficial match in Vancouver on the way home, beating British Colombia 63–5, and in 1936 they played an unofficial match in Brazil. In 1950 the Lions stopped over in Colombo on the way to Australia, beating Ceylon (now Sri Lanka) 44–6 and in 1959 the Lions played two matches in Canada, edging past British Columbia in Vancouver before smashing Eastern Canada in Toronto. They were back in North America seven years later, playing two matches in Canada on the way home from their miserable 1966 tour of New Zealand – it wasn't much better in the freezing north, the Lions losing to British Columbia in Vancouver before scraping past the Canucks national side 19–8 in Toronto. Matches were even staged against an East African XV in Nairobi in 1955 and 1962 and the Lions were also beaten 25–21 by Fiji in Suva in 1977.

— LIONS RECORDS: MOST DROP GOALS ON A TOUR*

DGs	Name	Venue	Games	Year
9	David Watkins	Australia, NZ and Canada	21	1966
8	Barry John	Australia and New Zealand	17	1971
7	Craig Chalmers	Australia	6+1	1989
6	Ollie Campbell	New Zealand	11	1983
6	Reg Skrimshire	South Africa	22	1903

*All official matches played in all countries including tests

— THE KING SHOWS HIS DISPLEASURE —

Gerald Davies once scored four tries in a single match, the bad-tempered and violent 25–6 win over Hawke's Bay at Napier in 1971. Barry 'the King' John showed his contempt for the hosts' brutal tactics by at one stage sitting on the ball before clearing to touch. At another point he taunted the opposing forwards, offering the ball to the advancing Hawke's Bay players before booting it clear in disgust.

— LIONS RECORDS: MOST POINTS IN A TEST SERIES —

For:

Pts	Name	Venue	Tests	Year
41	Neil Jenkins	South Africa	3	1997
38	Gavin Hastings	New Zealand	3	1993
36	Jonny Wilkinson	Australia	3	2001
35	Tom Kiernan	South Africa	4	1968
30	Barry John	New Zealand	4	1971

Against:

Pts	Name	Venue	Tests	Year
46	Allan Hewson	New Zealand	4	1983
44	Matt Burke	Australia	2+1	2001
44	Dan Carter	New Zealand	2	2005
39	Don Clarke	New Zealand	4	1959
37	Michael Williment	New Zealand	4	1966
36	Michael Lynagh	Australia	3	1993

— THE SHIRT OFF HIS BACK —

The amateur era was still alive and well in 1966, when the Scottish Rugby Union insisted that the each of their Lions players returned the two blazers, playing kit and grey flannel trousers which they had been given before the five-month tour of Australia and New Zealand.

— THE LION TURNED BISHOP —

The Oxford University and Lions forward Walter Carey enjoyed the 1896 tour of South Africa so much that he decided to stay on, eventually becoming the Bishop of Bloemfontein and coining the Barbarians' motto, "Rugby is a game for gentlemen in all classes but bad sports in no classes." He also said, "I reckon that if Hitler had been a rowing Blue or a rugger Blue history would have been different."

— A VERY SCOTTISH OCCASION —

The opening test of the 1903 tour to South Africa saw a unique line-up of referee and captains in that all three were Scots. The Springbok skipper, Alex Frew, was a doctor from Kilmarnock and had won a Triple Crown playing for Scotland under Mark Morrison. He had then emigrated to the Transvaal.

The Lions captain was Morrison himself, who had been first capped as a teenager and became Scotland skipper in 1899, going on to stay in the post until 1905, during which time he led Scotland to Triple Crowns in 1901 and 1903.

The referee was Bill Donaldson, a former Loretto man and Oxford Blue who won six caps for Scotland in the 1890s and was the first man to score at Scotland's new Inverleith home.

The test ended in a 10–10 draw, with Frew scoring one of the two Springbok tries. The second test was drawn, with the Springboks winning the third they didn't lose another home series for 55 years.

— TRAVELLING HEAVY —

The 1997 Lions to South Africa took 2.5 tons of luggage on tour with them.

— HOME SWEET HOME —

When the Lions drew 25–25 with Argentina at the Millennium Stadium in Cardiff before departing for New Zealand in 2005, it was only the third official Lions match held on British soil and the sixth in all. Apart from the draw against the Pumas, the Lions' two other 'official' matches in which they were at full strength were against the Barbarians at Twickenham in 1977 and against a Rest of the World XV in Cardiff in 1986.

The 1977 match almost didn't take place as the players initially threatened to boycott it when their wives and partners were not invited to attend. However, the organisers of the game, a charity fund-raiser held as part of the Queen's silver jubilee celebrations, eventually relented and the Lions went on to beat a stellar Baa-Baas line-up featuring JPR Williams, Gerald Davies, Gareth Edwards, Jean-Pierre Rives and Jean-Claude Skrela 23–14.

The 1986 match against the Rest of the World was, like the Argentina match, designed as a warm-up fixture ahead of the tour to South Africa. With the political climate turning decisively against sporting links with the apartheid-era regime, the tour was called off although the game, which doubled as a celebration match to mark the International Rugby Board's centenary, went ahead; the home side winning 15–7.

The most recent of the unofficial Lions outings in the northern hemisphere was in Paris in 1989 as part of the French Republic's anniversary celebrations when a side missing several of the key men who toured Australia, including captain Finlay Calder, was beaten 29–27.

The remaining two unofficial matches took place at the Arms Park, the first when the Lions beat Cardiff 14–12 in 1951 and the second in 1955 when a 'Lions' side without big-names such as Tony O'Reilly, Jeff Butterfield, Phil Davies, Dickie Jeeps, Bryn Meredith and Jim Greenwood beat a Welsh XV 20–17 in a match staged to mark the 75th anniversary of the Welsh Rugby Union.

— MYSTIC DOUG —

The manager of the 1971 Lions, Scot Dr Doug Smith, predicted before the tour left the UK that the Lions would win two tests, draw one and lose one. He was spot on.

— THE LIONS ON TOUR: 1955
(SOUTH AFRICA & KENYA) —

In South Africa: P24, W18, L5, D1, Pts 418–271
In Kenya: P1, W1, Pts 39–12
Tests: W23–22 (Johannesburg), L9–25 (Cape Town), W9–6 (Pretoria),
L8–22 (Port Elizabeth)

While the 1950 tourists charmed New Zealand and Australia with
their commitment to running rugby, they nevertheless failed to win a
test match. The 1955 Lions not only played sublime rugby, but also
did it while winning, eventually sharing the series 2–2.

Robin Thompson's side exploded the myth of Springbok
superiority, doing so with smiles on their faces. From the moment they
landed, they won hearts and minds, instantly being dubbed 'the
Singing Lions' after Cliff Morgan led an impromptu 30-minute sing-
song at Johannesburg Airport to entertain the thousands of fans who
greeted their arrival (see *The Singing Lions*, page 100).

The Welsh fly-half was also a huge hit on the park, spearheading
a Lions back division that ran whatever ball it was given, no matter
how unpromising the situation. If anything, the 1955 Lions backs were
arguably even more talented than the class of '50, with Morgan and
three Englishmen, uncapped scrum-half Dickie Jeeps and centres Jeff
Butterfield and Phil Davies, providing pace and guile in abundance.

However, the undoubted star of the show was rampaging Irish
sensation Tony O'Reilly. Barely 19, the flame-haired winger scored 16
tries in 15 matches, including two in the tests as he went on to establish
himself as the most effective wing ever to play for the Lions.

The Lions contained gritty and athletic forwards such as Wales
hooker Bryn Meredith, lock Rhys Williams and hard-tackling Scottish
flanker Jim Greenwood, but they weren't set up to go head to head
with the Springbok bruisers so played it fast and loose. The result
was four incredible tests in which the rapier of the Lions met the
bludgeon of the Springboks.

The first test remains one of the best known in Lions folklore,
with the 14-man Lions at one stage defending a 23–11 lead in the
second half in front of 105,000 spectators, only to have to rely on
Springbok fullback Jack van der Schyff missing an injury time
conversion to win the game by a point (See *The Greatest Lions
Matches 3*, page 37). South Africa roared back in the second test,
with Tom van Vollenhoven scoring a hat-trick, but in the third the

Lions played it tight for once, winning 9–6 through a try and drop goal from Butterfield. Although the Springboks outscored the exhausted, injury-ravaged Lions by five tries to two in the final test to square the series, it was a memorable tour.

Backs: Fullbacks: A Cameron (Glasgow HSFP and Scotland), AG Thomas (Llanelli and Wales) Centres and wings: J Butterfield (Northampton and England), WPC Davies (Harlequins and England), G Griffiths* (Cardiff and Wales), H Morris (Cardiff and Wales), AJF O'Reilly (Old Belvedere and Ireland), AC Pedlow (Queen's Univ, Belfast and Ireland), JP Quinn (New Brighton and England), AR Smith (Cambridge Univ and Scotland), FD Sykes (Northampton and England) Fly-halves and scrum-halves: DGS Baker (Old Merchant Taylors and England), REG Jeeps (Northampton), T Lloyd (Maesteg and Wales), CI Morgan (Cardiff and Wales), JE Williams (Old Millhillians and England)
Forwards: T Elliot (Gala and Scotland), JT Greenwood (Dunfermline and Scotland), R Higgins (Liverpool and England), HF McLeod (Hawick and Scotland), BV Meredith (Newport and Wales), CC Meredith (Neath and Wales), ETS Michie (Aberdeen Univ and Scotland), TE Reid (Garryowen and Ireland), RJ Robins (Pontypridd and Wales), R Roe (Lansdowne and Ireland), RCC Thomas (Swansea and Wales), RH Thompson (Instonians and Ireland, captain), RH Williams (Llanelli and Wales), WO Williams (Swansea and Wales), DS Wilson (Met Police and England)
(* replacement)
Managers: JAE Siggins, DE Davies (assistant)

— LEAGUE LIONS —

Ian McGeechan and Jim Telfer knew that the short tour of South Africa in 1997 – the first Lions tour since the game had gone professional – would need to be run with the utmost professionalism. So wherever possible they chose former rugby league players, taking six in all, of whom all four backs – Scott Gibbs, Allan Bateman, John Bentley, and Alan Tait – played in at least one test (Scott Quinnell was injured, while prop David Young was an invaluable dirt-tracker). The other ex-league player to tour with the Lions was in 2001, when Jason Robinson scored a try in the first test win in Brisbane.

— TRUE COLOURS —

The Lions jerseys may have been red for well over half a century, but it wasn't always so. Indeed, when in 1888 cricket entrepreneur Arthur Shrewsbury promoted the first expedition to Australia and New Zealand he demanded "something that would be good material and yet take them by storm out here". What he got was the first Lions jersey – thick red, white and blue hoops, worn above knee-length white shorts and dark socks.

The format changed slightly on the next two tours, which took the Lions to South Africa in 1891 and 1896. This time the red, white and blue scheme was retained, but with red and white hooped jerseys and dark blue shorts.

In 1899, the red, white and blue was back for the tourists' return to Australia, the blue used in thick hoops and the red and white in thin bands. England wore an updated version of this jersey in their commemorative test against Australia in Sydney in 1999, exactly 100 years after the Reverend Matthew Mullineux's early British tourists landed. The same kit was adopted in 1904 for the next tour to Australia and New Zealand, while the kit for the 1903 South Africa tour was once again the familiar red and white.

The first major change of format and colours came in 1908 when, with the Scottish and Irish unions declining to be involved, an Anglo-Welsh squad toured Australia and New Zealand wearing red jerseys with a thick white band that reflected the combination of the countries.

Two years later though, and with the Scots back in the fold, Dr Tom Smyth's 1910 tour to South Africa saw the introduction of the blue shirts that were to remain in place until the 1950 tour. There were variations though: in 1910 the dark blue jerseys with a single lion-rampant crest were accompanied by white shorts and red socks, while in 1924 the first side of the inter-war period returned to South Africa with the same blue shirts, but with shorts to match and a crest that was the forerunner of the four-quartered badge worn today.

The blue shirt caused a huge amount of controversy when the Lions returned to New Zealand in 1930 after a hiatus of 22 years because it clashed with the Kiwis' famous All Black shirts, and the convention in rugby (unlike soccer) is that the home side changes to accommodate its 'guests'. Only after a long squabble did the New Zealanders agree to change for the tests, the All Blacks becoming the All Whites for the first time.

And not all members of the Lions were completely happy with their own kit. Irish lock George Beamish led a delegation that said that if the blue shirt represented Scotland, the white shorts England and the red socks with white turnovers Wales, where was the green of Ireland? In the end, they accepted a compromise whereby the side added a green flash to the socks, but in practice it didn't stay in place in the heat of battle. The point had been made though and from 1938 onwards the green turnover has been a constant feature of the Lions strip.

Although the blue jersey survived through to the 1938 tour, it was on borrowed time, and when Karl Mullen's Lions returned to New Zealand in 1950 they avoided a repeat of the 1930 colour-clash controversy by adopting the red shirts, white shorts and dark blue and green socks that they still wear today.

Although the strip has remained largely unchanged since 1950, in 1993 the name of the manufacturer was included, and since then first Nike and then Adidas have had prominent branding, as have the main sponsors – Scottish Provident in 1997, NTL in 2001 and Zurich in 2005 – across the shirt front. HSBC will be the shirt sponsor for the 2009 tour to South Africa.

— KICKING FROM DISTANCE —

The longest drop goal scored by a Lion in a test match was teenage prodigy Lewis Jones' 50-metre effort in the first test victory against Australia in 1950. Another monstrous and notable effort was JPR Williams' 40-metre drop goal in the final test of the 1971 tour at Eden Park, Auckland which secured the 14–14 draw (and with it the 2–1 series win for the Lions). The Welshman's superb kick equalled Charles Grieve's famous 40-metre effort in the last test of the 1938 tour of South Africa, which was only given because the Springbok players sportingly indicated to the out-of-position referee that it had cleared the bar.

The longest kicks scored against the Lions were a 50-metre drop from a penalty by Springbok Roy Dryburgh in the third test in 1955, followed by Allan Hewson in 1983 when the All Black fullback kicked a 45–metre match-winning dropped-goal in the final minute of the first test.

— THE GREATEST LIONS MATCHES: 5 —

New Zealand 3, Lions 13
Third test
31st July 1971, Wellington

If the Lions had won the first test through epic defence and Barry John's pinpoint kicking, the third test win was a masterclass in how to get a match won early and then close it out with the minimum of fuss. By the end of the first quarter the Lions had blitzed the All Blacks, scoring 13 points to none and establishing a match-winning lead. As New Zealand skipper Colin Meads conceded, "We were beaten up front and we were beaten behind."

The key to the Lions' unstoppable start was the simple fact that captain John Dawes won the toss. It was blowing a gale that day in Wellington, and the Lions knew that they needed to put points on the board and make the jittery Kiwis chase the game. That is exactly what they did. Playing into a brisk breeze, Laurie Mains struggled to clear his lines and Barry John stroked over a drop goal within three minutes.

Five minutes later Gareth Edwards scampered down the blindside after the All Blacks had lost control of a bouncing ball at the tail of the line-out before feeding wing Gerald Davies for a try. Just to prove that everything was going their way, Barry John's touchline conversion crept in via a post. The match was effectively over after just 17 minutes when Edwards used all his strength in a bullocking run off the back of another line-out to go deep into All Black territory before offloading to John, who had little more to do than flop over the line before converting his own try.

With the Lions' thin red line as impenetrable as it had been in the first test at Carisbrook, the All Blacks had to settle for just one second half try from Mains, and never looked like clawing their way back into a game played at a frantic pace. With the 13–3 win came an unassailable 2–1 lead in the series, which is how it remained after a drawn fourth test in Auckland for the Lions' first – and so far only – series win in New Zealand.

— FORWARD POWER —

The 1977 Lions forwards were so much stronger than their Kiwi counterparts at the scrum that in the fourth and deciding test the All Blacks elected to scrummage with just three forwards to stop themselves being pushed off their own ball by the Lions. The All Blacks still won, beating the Lions 10–9 to make it a 3–1 series win thanks to No8 Laurie Knight's late winning try after he picked up on Peter Wheeler's fumble when hit by a sledgehammer tackle from flanker Graham Mourie.

In fairness, the Lions front five in that final test was a scrummaging unit to be compared with any in the game: Fran Cotton, Peter Wheeler and Graham Price in the front row, and Gordon Brown and Bill Beaumont in the second row.

— DOUBLE TRAGEDY —

Uncapped Heriot's FP centre Roy Kinnear played in all four matches of the 1924 tour to South Africa despite not having been able to force his way into the Grand Slam Scotland side, and although he went on to win three caps for Scotland, he left to join Wigan RLFC, winning the Challenge Cup and representing Great Britain RL against Australia at Hull in 1929.

When war broke out, union and league players were allowed to join ranks to play in fund-raising services matches and Kinnear tragically died on the pitch in just such a game at the age of 38.

His son, the comedian and actor of the same name, also died in tragic circumstances in 1988, falling off his horse during the filming of *The Return of the Musketeers* in Spain.

— TEST TRIBUTE —

The 2001 Lions wore black armbands in the second test in Melbourne after the death of their popular kitman, Anton Toia, who suffered a heart attack while swimming in the sea off Coffs Bay in the week after the first test.

— GREATEST LIONS XV: MIKE TEAGUE (BLINDSIDE FLANKER) —

Mike Teague

Mike Teague earns his Dream XV spurs despite playing in just two tests, but what tests they were. With Teague injured and unable to play, the Wallabies had ransacked the Lions pack in the first test in 1989, comprehensively winning the forward battle and beating the tourists 30–12. Teague had been the Lions' standout player in the early provincial tussles, and with his shoulder recovered he came back into the test side. Once there, he led from the front as he inspired the Lions pack, which dismantled the Aussies in one of the most brutal Lions Tests ever before going on to win the third test to take the series.

It would be an exaggeration to lay all the credit for the turnaround at Teague's door – Wade Dooley, Rob Andrew, Scott Hastings and Jerry Guscott also came in – but there is no doubt that Teague's hard-driving play, strength in the close-quarter work and hard-nosed approach to confronting the Wallabies galvanised a pack that had seriously under-performed in the first test. Such was Teague's impact that he was made the Lions player of the series, an accolade that surprised no-one.

After helping England to the 1991 World Cup final, the Gloucester man also made the 1993 tour but failed to make the test team, serving as understudy to the Lions' best player, fellow English back row man Ben Clarke.

Teague wins his place in the Dream Lions XV ahead of (in order) Roger Uttley, Derek Quinnell, Lawrence Dallaglio, Alun Pask, John O'Driscoll and Ben Clarke.

Mike Teague stats
Born: 8th October 1960
Tours: 1989
Tests: 1989 Aus 2, 3
27 caps for England, 1985–93
Club: Gloucester

— 'LOUSY LOVERS' —

The 1977 Lions were not a happy crew and were unpopular with their hosts. The Kiwi press, still smarting from the treatment meted out to Keith Murdoch over the notorious Angel Hotel incident of 1972/73 (the All Black prop smacked a bouncer in Cardiff and got sent home in disgrace after some fruity coverage in the British press), weighed in against the tourists. The Auckland paper *The Truth* ripped into them. "The Lions made a great pack – of animals. The touring British Isles rugby side is a disgrace to its members and their homeland. There has been only one word to describe their behaviour since the team arrived here: disgusting."

The 1977 Lions also had to put up with more prurient tabloid exposes. In an infamous kiss-and-tell, Kiwi groupie 'Wanda from Wanganui' claimed to have slept with four of the Lions and alleged that they were all rubbish in bed. "They're Lousy Lovers" ran the screaming headline in the *Sunday News*, with the New Zealander claiming that: "I found them boring, self-centred, ruthless, always on the make and anything but exciting bedmates . . . give me the down-to-earth Kiwi male any day".

This does beg the question, however, as to why she kept coming back for more.

— LIONS TWICE OVER —

Only nine Lions players who subsequently went north to rugby league have become Lions at both union and league. Newport wing Jack Morley was the first in the 1930s after he joined Wigan, and he has been followed since the war by fellow Welshmen Lewis Jones, Terry Price, David Watkins, Maurice Richards and John Bevan, plus Englishman Bev Risman, Scot Roy Kinnear, and, most recently, Scot Alan Tait.

— THE LIONS ON TOUR: 1959
(AUSTRALIA, NEW ZEALAND & CANADA) —

In Australia: P6, W5, L1, Pts 174–70
In New Zealand: P25, W20, L5, Pts 582–266
In Canada: P2, W2, Pts 86–17
Tests: Won 17–6 (Brisbane), W24–3 (Sydney); L17–18 (Dunedin);
L8–11 (Wellington), L8–22 (Christchurch), W6–9 (Auckland)

With a side containing many of the greats from 1955 and some talented additions in the backs, the Lions arrived with the same all-out attacking philosophy that made the 1950 and 1955 tours such a success. However, although they beat Australia twice and lost just three provincial matches (to New South Wales, Otago and Canterbury), they lost the test series 3–1 thanks largely to the incredible kicking of All Black fullback Don Clarke and the vagaries of the country's referees.

New Zealand's public felt immense disquiet at the way their side won the series. At the end of the first test in Dunedin, in which the Lions outplayed their hosts but were beaten 18–17 thanks to six Clarke penalties to three Lions tries, the home crowd chanted "Red! Red! Red!" as the enterprising Lions pressed for the winning try.

Ronnie Dawson's Lions were immensely popular. Many of the most gifted players from 1955 – backs Tony O'Reilly, Dickie Jeeps and Jeff Butterfield, and key forwards Bryn Meredith and Rhys Williams – toured in 1959, and they were joined by a quartet of swashbuckling young backs in Scots fullback Ken Scotland, powerhouse Irish centre David Hewitt and Englishmen Peter Jackson and Bev Risman, plus three tough forwards in Irishman Syd Millar, Scotland prop Hugh McLeod and Welsh flanker John Faull.

The Lions cut a swathe through New Zealand, running up big scores against top sides and scoring an average of 25 points per match, more than any previous Lions. O'Reilly was again the star, creating yet another try-scoring record with his 22 touchdowns, yet he was pushed hard by wing Jackson, who scored 19 tries, including two in his three tests.

The embittered Lions felt that, but for the home referees, they would have at least drawn the series and might well have won it. The second test was lost 11–8 thanks to a spectacular try from Clarke to two from the injury-ravaged Lions, and although the third was a resounding 22–8 defeat, the Lions roused themselves in the fourth to win 9–6, an emphatic three tries to nil victory in which the three buccaneers of Jackson, O'Reilly and Risman each claimed a try.

LIONS KITS
1888-2005

1888

1891 & 1896

1899

1903

1904

1908

1910

1924

1930 & 1936

1938

1950 – 1989

1993

1997

2001

2005

Backs: Fullbacks: TJ Davies (Llanelli and Wales), KJF Scotland, (Cambridge Univ and Scotland) Centres and wings: NH Brophy (UC Dublin and Ireland), J Butterfield (Northampton and England), D Hewitt (Queen's Univ, Belfast and Ireland), PB Jackson (Coventry and England), AJF O'Reilly (Old Belvedere and Ireland), WM Patterson* (Sale), MJ Price (Pontypool and Wales), MC Thomas (Newport and Wales), GH Waddell (Cambridge Univ and Scotland), JRC Young (Oxford Univ and England) Halfbacks: S Coughtrie (Edinburgh Acads and Scotland), MAF English (Limerick Bohemians and Ireland), JP Horrocks-Taylor* (Leicester and England), REG Jeeps (Northampton and England), AA Mulligan* (Wanderers, London Irish and Ireland), ABW Risman (Manchester Univ and England).

Forwards: A Ashcroft (Waterloo and England), AR Dawson (Wanderers and Ireland, capt), WR Evans (Cardiff and Wales), J Faull (Swansea and Wales), RWD Marques (Harlequins and England), HF McLeod (Hawick and Scotland), BV Meredith (Newport and Wales), S Millar (Ballymena and Ireland), HJ Morgan (Abertillery and Wales), NAA Murphy (Cork Constitution and Ireland), WA Mulcahy (UC Dublin and Ireland), R Prosser (Pontypool and Wales), GK Smith (Kelso and Scotland), BGM Wood (Garryowen and Ireland), RH Williams (Llanelli and Wales).

(* replacements)

Managers: AW Wilson, OB Glasgow (assistant).

— LIONS RECORDS: MOST PENALTY GOALS ON A TOUR* —

PGs	Name	Venue	Games	Year
29	Phil Bennett	New Zealand and Fiji	16	1977
28	Barry John	Australia and New Zealand	17	1971
27	Andy Irvine	South Africa and Rhodesia	14+1	1974
24	Gavin Hastings	New Zealand	8+1	1993
22	Ollie Campbell	New Zealand	11	1983
22	Neil Jenkins	South Africa	6+2	1997
22	Tom Kiernan	South Africa and Rhodesia	12+1	1968

*All official matches played in all countries including tests

— DOOLEY'S DOWNER —

England lock Wade Dooley's Lions career ended on a real low in New Zealand in 1993. The lifelong ambition of the Preston policeman, who had been a key player in the Lions side which recovered from losing the first test to beat the Wallabies 2–1 in 1989, had been to face the All Blacks for the Lions, and right at the tail end of his international career he was chosen to tour New Zealand in 1993.

The tour started well, with Dooley playing his part in wins over North Harbour, North Auckland, Canterbury and in a spectacular comeback win over the Maoris before disaster struck: a week before the first test, Dooley's father died. The big lock rushed back to Lancashire, but both he and tour manager Geoff Cooke, as well as Four Home Unions Committee secretary Bob Weighill fully expected him to be back. It was not to be, however: despite Weighill having bought him a return ticket, the committee said that he was no longer covered by their insurance and could no longer play. Rather than fulfil the invitation to go back and watch the tour as a spectator, a distraught Dooley opted instead to stay at home, Cooke adding that it was, "an appalling way to treat a person who has given such a lot to the game."

If there was a silver lining, it was in captain Gavin Hastings's admission that Dooley's treatment galvanised the squad and bolstered team morale, which was flagging after a 37–24 cuffing at the hands of Otago. Dooley's misfortune also turned out to be the break one young second row – a callow former All Blacks Colt called Martin Johnson – needed. The Leicester player was sent out as Dooley's replacement and played four games on tour, including the last two tests.

— NOT SO PROUD LIONS —

The first British Lions side to have lost more matches than it won was Ronald Cove-Smith's 1924 side to South Africa. The first to fail to win a test match was Mark Morrison's 1903 tourists, who drew the first two tests and were beaten 8–0 by South Africa in the third test.

— HANGING ON THE LINE —

"Can we have out ball back please"

When the Lions played Wellington on the 1888 tour, not only were there tree stumps and roots running across the pitch, but there were also telephone wires running overhead across the field of play. At one stage play had to be held up while a ladder was fetched after the ball became entangled in those wires.

— TALLEST AND HEAVIEST LIONS —

Officially the tallest man to play for the Lions was 6ft 10in England second row Martin Bayfield, who was a key line-out forward in New Zealand in 1993. The heaviest are two props, Irishman John Hayes and Englishman Phil Vickery, who both weighed in at 122kgs (19st 2lb) in 2005. The shortest Lion was 5ft 4in Matthew Mullineux in 1896 and 1899. The lightest was 9st 9lb Herbert Whitley in 1924.

— BROTHERS IN ARMS —

- **William and Robert Burnet (1888):** The first pair of brothers to play for the Lions were the Burnet brothers from Hawick who travelled to New Zealand and Australia on the 1888 'Originals' tour, although as there were no tests in 1888 they both remained uncapped.

- **William and Edward Bromet (1891):** The first brothers to be capped together for the Lions were two English brothers from Tadcaster, England cap William Bromet, who played for Oxford University, and his older brother Edward, a Cambridge University player who was to remain uncapped. William played in all three tests in 1891, while Edward only played in the second and third.

- **Randolph (1891) and Ferdy Aston (1896):** Randolph Aston was a member of the 1891 Lions tour, but his younger brother Ferdy ended up playing against the Lions rather than for them, captaining the Springboks against the Lions with some distinction in the 1896 series.

- **Louis and Jim Magee (1896):** No brothers have played for the Lions with more distinction than the supremely gifted Irish halfback Louis Magee and his brother Jim, two members of the Bective Rangers dynasty. Louis played in all four tests in 1896, while Jim played just the second and fourth.

- **James and Joseph Wallace (1903):** Brothers James and Joseph Wallace, two Dublin Wanderers from Dromakeenan in Roscrea, toured South Africa together. While James went on to get 12 Ireland caps to his brother's two, it was Joseph who played in all three tests in 1903, while Joseph never won a Lions cap.

- **JP 'Ponty' and JP 'Tuan' Jones (1908):** The decision of the Scots and Irish not to tour in 1908 meant that the players were drawn from a smaller pool, and there were five former pupils from Christ's Brecon School, including Jack 'Ponty' Jones and Jack 'Tuan' Jones. Ponty played in all three tests, scoring the try in the 3–3 second test draw, while Tuan played in just the last two.

- **Teddy (1904) and Willie Morgan (1908):** The two brothers didn't play their club rugby together and nor did they ever tour abroad together. Medic Teddy was a threequarter who played for Guy's Hospital and London Welsh, while Willie was a Swansea forward.

- **HJ and WL Fraser (1930):** The two Merchistonians toured Argentina in 1910. HJ played one game in the centre and WL three games in the pack.

- **George (1930) and Charles Beamish (1936):** Ulsterman Charles toured Argentina in 1936 six years after his brother George had been the star forward on the 1930 tour to Argentina and New Zealand.
- **Jim (1983) and Finlay Calder (1989):** The two Scots were brothers, yet Jim had played his last test before Finlay played his first. Jim's only test was the third test defeat against New Zealand in 1983, but Finlay led the Lions to a series win in Australia in 1989. John Beattie, who came on as a replacement in the second test 1983, is the Calders' cousin.
- **Scott and Gavin Hastings (1989 and 1993):** Brothers Scott and Gavin Hastings made their Scotland debuts together in 1986 and are the only brothers to have gone on two tours together. Gavin captained the 1993 Lions and played in all three tests in 1989, while Scott played just the second and third tests in Australia in 1989, both of which the Lions won.
- **Rory (1989, 1993) and Tony Underwood (1993, 1997):** The Leicester wingers' careers overlapped briefly, but Tony didn't get a test in 1993, winning his only Lions cap in the series-clinching second test in South Africa in 1997. Rory played in all three tests in both 1989 and 1993.
- **Iain (1983) and Kenny Milne (1993):** Of the two Scottish front row players, only hooker Kenny won a Lions cap, gaining it in the first test in 1993.
- **Richard (1993), Paul (1997) and David Wallace (2001):** What a story. Three brothers make consecutive tours, all three being called on tour at the last minute as replacements for injured players. One's a wing, one an openside flanker, the other a prop – you couldn't make it up. The fairytale isn't complete, however, because the only one of the trio of Munstermen to be capped was Paul, coming from nowhere in the pecking order to play all three games in the triumphant 1997 tour of South Africa after only making the tour three weeks before it departed when Peter Clohessy withdrew injured.

— A MATTER OF HONOUR —

In 1908, well before the days of substitutes, Wellington skipper Freddy Roberts offered a substitute when Lions fullback John Jackett left the pitch injured, but the Lions refused such an offer as "against the spirit of the game".

— THE LIONS ON TOUR: 1962
(SOUTH AFRICA & KENYA) —

In South Africa: P24, W15, L5, D4, Pts 351–208
In Kenya: P1, W1, Pts 50–0
Tests: D3–3 (Johannesburg); L3–0 (Durban); L8–3 (Cape Town); L34–14 (Bloemfontein)

The 1962 tour was in marked contrast to what had come before. The Springboks had toured Britain in 1960–61, comfortably beating all four home unions, with their only 'test' defeat coming against a Barbarians side with a huge pack. So, with no backs to match those of the 1950s, the 1962 Lions were reliant on the biggest pack ever to leave these shores, including nine men over 15 stone (the 1955 party had three).

It turned out to be the same old story for the highly cerebral Arthur Smith's Lions, a case of what could have been. Although they only lost two provincial matches (to Northern Transvaal and Eastern Transvaal) and three of the four tests were hotly contested, they were a utilitarian side short on the flair of the sides of the 1950s.

With big beasts like Syd Millar, Keith Rowlands, Mike Campbell-Lamerton and Willie John McBride playing alongside Bryn Meredith, the hooker from 1950 and 1955, and Alun Pask, they certainly had the firepower to match a Springbok pack then at its peak. The Lions didn't take a step backwards, yet they lacked specialist flankers and struggled to win ball out wide or to provide quick ball. With a lack of genuine class behind the scrum, the result was a static side that found tries hard to come by.

The first test was a dull 3–3 wrestling contest enlivened only by excellent tries from John Gainsford and Lions centre DK Jones. The second test was little better, although the Lions forwards had the upper hand, the match ending in controversy when unsighted referee Ken Carlson failed to award what looked like a perfectly good pushover try from Keith Rowlands which would have cancelled out the Keith Oxlee penalty that gave the Springboks a 3–0 win.

Oxlee was again the match-winner in the third test when Lions fly-half Richard Sharp tried to run from his own line after a heel against the head and was forced to give a hospital pass to Jones, who was heavily tackled, Oxlee scoring and converting the try to make it 8–3. Oxlee, the star of the series, dominated the fourth test as the Springboks finally opened up, the Natal No10 breaking the Lions line time after time as the hosts won 34–14 largely thanks to Oxlee's 16 points and a spell after half-time in which they scored 13 points in five minutes.

Backs: Fullbacks: TJ Kiernan (Univ College Cork and Ireland), JG Wilcox (Oxford Univ and England) Centres and wings: DIE Bebb (Swansea and Wales), NH Brophy (Univ College Dublin and Ireland), RC Cowan (Selkirk and Scotland), JM Dee (Hartlepool Rovers and England), D Hewitt (Queen's Univ, Belfast and Ireland), WR Hunter (CIYMS and Ireland), DK Jones (Llanelli and Wales), AR Smith (Edinburgh Wanderers and Scotland, capt), MP Weston (Durham City and England) Fly-halves and scrum-halves: HJC Brown* (Blackheath and RAF), REG Jeeps (Northampton and England), A O'Connor (Aberavon and Wales), RAW Sharp (Oxford Univ and England), GH Waddell (London Scottish and Scotland).

Forwards: MJ Campbell-Lamerton (Army, Halifax and Scotland), GD Davidge* (Newport and Wales), J Douglas (Stewart's College FP and Scotland), HO Godwin* (Coventry and England), SAM Hodgson (Durham City and England), KD Jones (Cardiff and Wales), WJ McBride (Ballymena and Ireland), BV Meredith (Newport and Wales), S Millar (Ballymena and Ireland), HJ Morgan (Abertillery and Wales), WA Mulcahy (Bohemians and Ireland), D Nash (Ebbw Vale and Wales), AEI Pask (Abertillery and Wales), DP Rogers (Bedford and England), DMD Rollo (Howe of Fife and Scotland), KA Rowlands (Cardiff and Wales), TP Wright (Blackheath and England). (*replacements)

Managers: DB Vaughan, HR McKibbin (assistant)

— LIONS RECORDS: MOST TRIES IN A TEST SERIES —

For:

Tries	Name	Venue	Tests	Year
4	Willie Llewellyn	Australia	3	1904
4	JJ Williams	South Africa	4	1974
3	Jack Spoors	South Africa	3	1910
3	Carl Aarvold	New Zealand	4	1930
3	Jeff Butterfield	South Africa	4	1955
3	Gerald Davies	New Zealand	4	1971

Against:

5	Frank Mitchinson	New Zealand	3	1908
5	Theuns Briers	South Africa	4	1955
4	Tom van Vollenhoven	South Africa	4	1955
4	Ralph Caulton	New Zealand	3	1959
4	Stu Wilson	New Zealand	4	1983

— GREATEST LIONS XV: GARETH EDWARDS (SCRUM-HALF) —

Gareth Edwards

In a *Rugby World* poll of professional rugby players in 2003, Gareth Edwards was declared the greatest player of all time. It's certainly difficult to disagree, even if supporters of Colin Meads or John Eales might take issue with that verdict.

A Welsh-speaking miner's son from Gwaun-cae-Gurwen in West Wales, Edwards' precocious talent was picked up early, and he won the first of his 53 consecutive Welsh caps as a teenager, first captaining his country at the age of 20 years and seven months. In the ten seasons that he played for Wales, they won the Five Nations seven times and collected three Grand Slams. He was, in short, a phenomenon.

Edwards combined the incredible pace of a sprinter with the strength of a lightweight boxer and the diligence of an academic. Talent plus application was a potent mix that turned the most gifted Lion into the most accomplished of them all.

Edwards was lucky to play his rugby for club, country and Lions from 1968–72 with a sublime talent in Barry John. Although they didn't dominate the 1968 Lions tour as they had expected – John broke his collarbone 15 minutes into the first test while Edwards tore a hamstring before the second – it was a vital learning curve for Edwards who spent the enforced rest learning how to spin pass, in the process developing the best service in world rugby.

In New Zealand in 1971, Edwards was immense behind a pack that was often beaten. In particular his turbocharged service gave John the time he needed to dominate games with his cultured boot and immaculate playmaking. Edwards' duel with Sid Going was one of the highlights of the tour, as was his break down the narrow side in the third test that put in Gerald Davies for the decisive try.

If John dominated in 1971, behind a completely dominant pack in South Africa in 1974 it was Edwards who stole the show. After John's retirement in 1972, the scrum-half had taken on more of the decision-making role and he thrived. In tandem with fellow Welshmen, No8 Mervyn Davies and fly-half Phil Bennett, he conducted proceedings, the trio carving the Springboks apart with ruthless efficiency.

Edwards had a full armoury at his disposal, and now he had added faultless decision-making he was the main man for the Lions. His value was shown on several occasions, but three cameos that stick in the mind are the first test drop goal which broke the Springbok resistance, the scuttling break that carved out a try for JJ Williams and preserved the Lions' unbeaten provincial record against Orange Free State, and the powerful third test reverse pass that completely wrong-footed the Springbok defenders and gave Bennett all the time he needed to kick the drop goal that capped the 26–9 win.

The ultimate accolade comes from those who played with him. Willie John McBride described him as "the best scrum-half I have seen or am ever likely to see", while Englishman Fran Cotton, who toured with Edwards in 1974, said: "Gareth was the greatest rugby player I ever played with. I never lost a game when he was in the same team and in '74 he was at his absolute peak. He tormented the opposition."

The only pity is that he didn't tour with the 1977 Lions. Had he done so, they would surely have come home victorious.

Edwards wins his place in the Lions Dream XV ahead of (in order) Dickie Jeeps, Matt Dawson, Robert Jones and Roy Laidlaw.

Gareth Edwards stats
Born: 12th July 1947
Tours: 1968, 1971, 1974
Tests: 1968 SA 1, 2; 1971 NZ 1, 2, 3, 4; 1974 SA 1, 2, 3, 4
53 caps for Wales, 1967–78
Club: Cardiff

— ARMOURED UP —

Body armour may still be a contentious subject, but it is not a new one. During the 1959 Lions tour, post-match pictures of All Black second row forward 'Tiny' Hill wearing a leather-padded waistcoat caused a furore, especially when it transpired that he was one of seven Kiwis to have worn such protective devices – all with doctor's notes, as the NZRFU were keen to point out.

— AIRBOURNE LIONS —

Although the 1955 party to South Africa was the first to travel by air on a 36-hour journey that included changes in Zurich, Rome, Cairo, Khartoum, Nairobi, Entebbe and Johannesburg, a lone Lion had already entered the world of air travel five years earlier.

That first airborne Lion was Lewis Jones, the Welsh teenager who was sent out by plane as a replacement for George Norton when the Irishman broke his arm in New Zealand in 1950.

Jones managed to displace fullback Billy Cleaver almost immediately, and not only played in the fourth test in New Zealand but, in the first test in Australia, became the first (and so far only) Lions player to score a 'full house' in a test, when he scored two conversions, two penalties, a try and a drop goal, with the 50-metre drop goal the longest ever kicked by a Lion in a test match.

— PENALTY KING —

Gavin Hastings holds the record for the highest number of penalties in a Lions test match, scoring six against New Zealand in the first test in Christchurch in 1993. The highest number scored against the Lions is also six, by All Black Don 'The Boot' Clarke in the 18–17 first test win in Dunedin in 1959, and by Matt Burke for Australia in the 35–14 Wallaby victory in the second test in 2001.

— LIONS RECORDS: MOST PENALTY GOALS IN A TEST —

For:

6	Gavin Hastings	New Zealand (Christchurch)	12th Jun 1993
5	Tom Kiernan	South Africa (Pretoria)	8th Jun 1968
5	Tony Ward	South Africa (Cape Town)	31st May 1980
5	Gavin Hastings	Australia (Sydney)	15th Jul 1989
5	Neil Jenkins	South Africa (Durban)	28th Jun 1997
5	Neil Jenkins	South Africa (Cape Town)	21st Jun 1997

Against:

6	Matt Burke	Australia (Melbourne)	7th Jul 2001
6	Don Clarke	New Zealand (Dunedin)	17th Jul 1959
5	Dan Carter	New Zealand (Wellington)	2nd Jul 2005
5	Matt Burke	Australia (Sydney)	14th Jul 2001
5	Grant Fox	New Zealand (Christchurch)	12th Jun 1993

— DAI'S A SPRINGBOK —

DO Williams, the flying Springbok who scored two tries in the first test against the 1938 Lions, had two Welsh parents and was a Welsh speaker who answered to 'Dai'. It was his disallowed try in the third test that gave the Lions their first test win over the Springboks for 28 years.

— POPULAR ATTRACTION —

A cool 678,000 spectators watched the 1955 Lions tour in South Africa, including an estimated 105,000 for the first test at Ellis Park (the capacity was 95,000 but forged tickets were rife).

— KEEPING AN EYE OUT —

The eye of the Springbok

During the brutal third test in 1974, there was a shriek from one of the Springbok forwards. Johannes de Bruyn had lost his glass eye and the warring packs ceased fighting for a moment to find it in the mud, whereupon de Bruyn promptly popped it back in its socket.

"And there was Cyclops," said Brown, "with tufts of grass hanging from behind his eye. I stood in amazement, he just nodded."

Years later, with Brown in failing health, De Bruyn came to London for a fund-raising dinner, confirmed the story was true and presented his old adversary with the glass eye mounted on a carved wooden rugby ball.

— BANNED FOR BUYING A SUIT! —

The 1888 'Originals' side was made up almost exclusively of players from the north of England, which led to accusations that the tour was tainted by professionalism. Indeed, one of the players, Halifax's Jack Clowes, who was born in Philadelphia in the USA, was banned by the RFU for professionalism for accepting £15 from tour organisers Shaw and Shrewsbury to kit himself out with a suit for the tour. Although he toured, Shaw and Shrewsbury never dared play him, and on the party's return to London every member was required to sign an affidavit confirming that he had not been paid.

— THE LIONS ON TOUR: 1966
(AUSTRALIA, NEW ZEALAND & CANADA) —

In Australia: P8, W7, D1, Pts 202–48
In New Zealand: P25, W15, L8, D2, Pts 300–281
In Canada: P2, W1, L1, Pts 22–16
Tests: W11–8 (Sydney), W31–0 (Brisbane); L3–20 (Dunedin);
L12–16 (Wellington); L6–19 (Christchurch), L11–24 (Auckland)

Mike Campbell-Lamerton's Lions were the first to lose all four tests in a series, ensuring that 1966 is remembered as the nadir in the touring side's fortunes. Yet it had all started so well, the side's triumphant progress through Australia climaxing after eight games with a resounding 31–0 test victory. How did it go so wrong so quickly, with the team even enduring the indignity of defeat by British Columbia in Vancouver on the way home?

Much blame has been laid at the feet of Campbell-Lamerton, but the Scot was almost certainly a compromise and probably the wrong choice as skipper – not least because he couldn't be assured of his place in the side. A suicidal itinerary didn't help, nor did a staggering rate of injuries, or the fact that manager Des O'Brien left for a break in Fiji mid-tour as all fell apart, while coach John Robins damaged his achilles tendon in a charity match and hobbled around on crutches for most of the tour.

Yet the primary problem was that while the Lions had some talented players in forwards Willie John McBride, Jim Telfer, Delme Thomas, Noel Murphy and Alun Pask, and a set of useful backs spearheaded by star turns Dai Watkins and Mike Gibson, they were no match for one of the great All Blacks sides. That great rugby thinker Fred Allen could call on legends like Colin Meads, Ken Gray, Chris Laidlaw and one the best back rows of all time in Waka Nathan, Kel Tremain and Brian Lochore.

The Lions also bridled at the roughness of New Zealand rugby, and the tour was punctuated by rows over the levels of violence and by the harshness of the rucking. That guru of rucking play, Otago coach Vic Cavanagh, called the Lions "a nothing team", and while that was harsh, they won just 15 of their 25 matches in New Zealand and never came remotely near to winning the series. The closest they came to winning a test was the seond test in Wellington, when they led 9–8 at half-time in the rain and mud and could have turned the 16–12 defeat into a win had Delme Thomas's pass after a 50-yard run in the dying moments gone to hand. But the other three tests, with the home pack utterly dominant, were heavy defeats.

Backs: Fullbacks: TG Price* (Llanelli and Wales), D Rutherford (Gloucester and England), S Wilson (London Scottish and Scotland) Centres and wings: DIE Bebb (Swansea and Wales), FBK Bresnihan* (Wanderers and Ireland), AJW Hinshelwood (London Scottish and Scotland), DK Jones (Cardiff and Wales), CW McFadyean (Moseley and England), KF Savage (Northampton and England), JC Walsh (Sunday's Well and Ireland), SJ Watkins (Newport and Wales), MP Weston (Durham City and England) Fly-halves and scrum-halves: CMH Gibson (Cambridge Univ and Ireland), AR Lewis (Newport and Wales), D Watkins (Newport and Wales), RM Young (Queen's Univ, Belfast and Ireland).
Forwards: MJ Campbell-Lamerton (London Scottish and Scotland, capt), D Grant (Hawick and Scotland), KW Kennedy (CIYMS and Ireland), FAL Laidlaw (Melrose and Scotland), RA Lamont (Instonians and Ireland), WJ McBride (Ballymena and Ireland), RJ McLoughlin (Gosforth and Ireland), NAA Murphy (Cork Constitution and Ireland), CH Norris (Cardiff and Wales), AEI Pask (Abertillery and Wales), DL Powell (Northampton and England), B Price (Newport and Wales), GJ Prothero (Bridgend and Wales), JW Telfer (Melrose and Scotland), WD Thomas (Llanelli), D Williams (Ebbw Vale and Wales).
(* replacement)
Manager: DJ O'Brien **Coach:** JD Robins.

— REFS TO THE FOUR —

In 1971, Carwyn James refused to countenance the NZRFU's original choice of referee for the first test between the All Blacks and the Lions, claiming that the official had once lifted both arms in salutation after a successful Fergie McCormick penalty. Instead, he urged the host union to use John Pring, who performed so well that he became only the second (and last) referee to officiate at all four matches of a four-test series.

The first to manage this feat was Boet Neser, who refereed all four tests of the 1924 series between the Lions and South Africa. Neser was also his country's wicketkeeper and cricket captain in 1924/25 for the visit of England. A Rhodes scholar who represented Oxford University in the Varsity match as both a flanker and fly-half, he went on to referee nine Springbok rugby tests.

— THE GREATEST LIONS MATCHES: 6 —

South Africa 9, Lions 28
Second test
22nd June 1974, Pretoria

The Springboks said they were caught unawares in the first test at Newlands. They said the soggy underfoot conditions that led to a tryless game suited the British style of play. They said that it would be a very different game when the two sides met at altitude on the hard ground of Loftus Versfeld in the second test. How right they were.

Never before or since have the Springboks been taken apart in the way that they were in Pretoria, where the Lions outscored them by five tries to nil. Up front the tourists' piano-movers destroyed Hannes Marais' bewildered and outclassed footsoldiers, particularly in the scrums. Out among the concert pianists, a Lions back division bristling with talent scythed through the green-shirted defenders almost at will. It was a humbling experience for a nation that had grown used to the concept of Springbok invincibility.

The Lions halfbacks Gareth Edwards and Phil Bennett were at their best in this test, directing operations and continually stretching the Springboks' defences. The South African rearguard was working overtime in the first half, but wing JJ Williams still managed to score two tries, scooting down either wing, with Bennett converting the second. Gerald Bosch's dropped goal meant it was 10–3 at half-time.

The second half was a horror show for the Springboks. Bennett was imperious, with the try he scored from 50 yards out, where he breezed around fullback Ian McCallum as if he wasn't there, bringing the crowd to its feet. There were further tries from Gordon Brown and centre Dick Milliken, plus a drop goal from centre Ian McGeechan and a penalty from Bennett. Bosch kicked two penalties for South Africa, but they were little consolation for the most devastating and comprehensive defeat ever inflicted upon the Springboks.

— LIONS ON FILM —

The 1955 tour was the first in which the tests were filmed and then shown back in Britain.

— GREATEST LIONS XV: BARRY JOHN (FLY-HALF) —

Barry John

In 1971, he scored 30 of the tourists' 48 test points as the Lions won their first ever series in New Zealand. The New Zealand public were in no doubt they were witnessing a genius at work and christened him 'The King', so highly did they rate him. Yet Barry John almost never made the tour that made his name.

John had broken his nose against France in that year's Five Nations and didn't want to tour, so when the letter of invitation arrived he literally ignored it. It took hours of persuasion from coach Carwyn James to get John to change his mind. No-one else could have swayed John, but both the fly-half and James were from the small village of Cefneithin near Llanelli and there was a bond there. Even then, James had to agree that John could train when he wanted and play when he wanted. Ten days before the team assembled, John finally informed James he would go.

John had already toured with the Lions, raising expectations in 1968 when the South Africans could see how potent a partnership he would form with Gareth Edwards. Yet injury intervened, with a desperate tackle from legendary Springbok flanker Jan Ellis tripping John over, the fly-half breaking his collarbone just 15 minutes into the first test.

John had the unshakeable self-belief and confidence of the truly gifted and never believed he had anything to prove in New Zealand. He simply went out and did what James asked him to. In the first test, that was tormenting the great fullback Fergie McCormick, who was so humiliated by John that he never played for the All Blacks again.

But John was more than a kicker (in fact, he even wasn't the number one kicker for his club or country and disliked kicking, but deferred to James as ever). John dominated every facet of a tour in which his forwards were often struggling. With Edwards providing such quick ball that he had time to choose his options, he put on a stunning show of bravura decision-making: one minute he would put in well-placed grubber kick, the next it would be a quick flat pass, or he would sidestep and shimmy his way through the tightest of gaps.

At just 5ft 9in and 12 stone, John relied on skill and subtlety rather than brute force, a fact that was never better demonstrated than in his almost single-handed 47–9 dismantling of Wellington, who were at that time New Zealand's provincial champions. When John played well, so did the Lions, and after he had dominated the first test he combined with Edwards in the third for a sublime try, kicked two touchline conversions and the drop-goal that started the 13–3 rout.

However, almost as soon as he burst into the public consciousness, he was gone. After the 1971 tour, John couldn't handle the media pressure and public adoration. "I never sought adulation," he said. After three matches of the 1972 Five Nations he quit, aged just 27.

It was a savage blow to both the Lions and Wales. "He played rugby on a different plane from anyone else I ever saw," said Mervyn Davies. "He was on a different, superior, wavelength."

John earned his place in the Greatest Lions XV by beating (in order) Phil Bennett, Jackie Kyle, Cliff Morgan, Gregor Townsend, Bev Risman, Rob Andrew, David Watkins and Ollie Campbell.

Barry John: Born: 6th January 1945
Tours: 1968 & 1971
Tests: 1968 SA 1; 1971 NZ 1, 2, 3, 4
25 caps for Wales, 1966–72
Club: Cardiff

— LIONS RECORDS: MOST POINTS IN A TOURING GAME —

For:

37	Alan Old	v South West Districts	29th May 1974
27	Tim Stimpson	v Northern Free State	1st Jul 1997
26	Tim Stimpson	v Emerging Springboks	17th Jun 1997
26	Ronan O'Gara	v Western Australia	8th Jun 2001

Against :

23	Manny Edmonds	v Australia A	19th Jun 2001
21	Marty Roebuck	v New South Wales	24th Jun 1989
20	Casper Steyn	v Northern Transvaal	7th Jun 1997
20	Jannie de Beer	v Free State Cheethas	24th Jun 1997
20	Federico Todeschini	v Argentina	23rd May 2005

— THE SINGING LIONS —

The 1955 Lions became known as 'the Singing Lions'. Not only were the double act of Tony O'Reilly and Cecil Pedlow always putting on shows for the party and their hosts, but there were a dozen Welshmen on board. The nametag was bestowed when the Lions arrived at Jan Smuts airport in Johannesburg and found a huge crowd waiting and responded with an impromptu rendition of the Afrikaans anthem *Sarie Marais*, as taught to them by choirmaster Cliff Morgan. On their departure after a drawn series, the Lions sang *Sarie Marias, Sospan Bach* and *Now is the Hour* to the thousands of South Africans who turned up to wave them off.

The Springboks were also in good voice on their way to the first test, a fact that Danie Craven apparently believed led to their loss on the basis that a team which sings before a test is destined to weep after it (he banned the Boks from singing for the rest of the tour). Whether pre-match singing is really a sign of a lack of motivation is a moot point, but Craven banned singing thereafter anyway.

Convinced that the British press were spying on the Springboks training sessions, he also made them train at night before the crucial third test: they lost.

— THE LIONS ON TOUR: 1968
(SOUTH AFRICA & RHODESIA) —

P20, W15, L4, D1, Pts 377–181
Tests: L20–25 (Pretoria), D6–6 (Port Elizabeth), L6–11 (Cape Town),
L6–19 (Johannesburg)

The 1968 Lions marked a return to the free-running sides of the fifties and laid the foundations for the successful tours of 1971 and 1974. SARB President Danie Craven rated them an excellent team and Tom Kiernan's outfit had enough quality to challenge the Springboks with some hope of success. Yet the fact that they came up short was not simply because they were hampered by injuries.

Although they still managed to be highly competitive in the test series, it was only Kiernan's boot that kept the Lions in touch. In truth, the Springboks were relatively comfortable winners. Away from the tests, the Lions won all but one of their provincial games, most with something to spare, their only defeat coming when Bob Hiller's dirt-trackers were outmuscled by a strong Transvaal outfit four days before the first test.

The squad contained some stellar talents, such as backs Barry John, Gareth Edwards, Mike Gibson, Gerald Davies and Maurice Richards, and forwards such as Willie John McBride, Jim Telfer, Delme Thomas, Mick Doyle, John Taylor, Rodger Arneil and Ken Goodall. However, the backs were devastated by injuries, with Edwards, John, Gibson and Davies failing to play a single test match together, while the forwards met a Springbok pack containing the legendary Frik Du Preez and peerless breakaways Jan Ellis, Tommy Bedford and Piet Greyling. Behind the scrum, Dawie De Villiers and Jannie Engelbrecht were in their pomp.

Still, the scores in the first three tests were all close, even if the Lions forwards were hanging on by their fingertips and their backs outscored by eight tries to one over the series, Kiernan's 35 points with the boot their main weapon (he scored all their test points except for one McBride try). The first test ended 25–20, but the Lions were well beaten in front of 75,000 spectators and lost Barry John, their main creative force, to a broken collarbone. The second test was drawn 6–6 and was notable for the Lions' heroic tackling and for refereeing so one-eyed that it ruined the game.

After a riot in Springs, where John O'Shea became the first Lion to be sent off and was pelted with fruit by the crowd (see *Dobbo is First To Go*, page 130), precipitating an all-in brawl, the Lions also lost the third test 11–6 and were blown away by the Springbok back row in the second half of the fourth test.

Backs: Fullbacks: R Hiller (Harlequins and England), TJ Kiernan (Cork Constitution and Ireland, capt) Centres and wings: FPK Bresnihan (Univ College Dublin and Ireland), TGR Davies (Cardiff and Wales), AJW Hinshelwood (London Scottish and Scotland), KS Jarrett (Newport and Wales), WK Jones (Cardiff and Wales), WH Raybould (London Welsh and Wales), MCR Richards (Cardiff and Wales), KF Savage (Northampton and England), JWC Turner (Gala and Scotland) Fly-halves and scrum-halves: GC Connell* (London Scottish and Scotland), GO Edwards (Cardiff and Wales), CMH Gibson (North of Ireland and Ireland), B John (Cardiff and Wales), RM Young (Queen's Univ, Belfast and Ireland)

Forwards: RJ Arneil (Edinburgh Accads and Scotland), MJ Coulman (Moseley and England), MG Doyle (Blackrock College and Ireland), KG Goodall* (City of Derry and Ireland), AL Horton (Blackheath and England), PJ Larter (Northampton and England), WJ McBride (Ballymena and Ireland), S Millar (Ballymena and Ireland), JP O'Shea (Cardiff and Wales), JV Pullin (Bristol and England), PK Stagg (Sale and Scotland), J Taylor (London Welsh and Wales), RB Taylor (Northampton and England), JW Telfer (Melrose and Scotland), WD Thomas (Llanelli and Wales), BR West* (Northampton and England), J Young (Harrogate and Wales)

(* replacements)

Manager: DK Brooks Coach: AR Dawson

— LIONS RECORDS: MOST DROP GOALS IN TEST MATCHES —

For:

DGs	Name	Tests	Year
2	Percy Bush	4	1904
2	David Watkins	6	1966
2	Barry John	5	1968–71
2	Phil Bennett	8	1974–77
2	Rob Andrew	5	1989–93

Against:

DGs	Name	Venue	Tests	Year
2	Macfarlane Herewini	New Zealand	4	1966

— VAN'S THE MAN —

Tom van Vollenhoven, the strapping Northern Transvaal wing who became the first Springbok ever to go to rugby league when he and Western Province wing Jan Prinsloo joined St Helens in 1956, is one of only three men ever to score a hat-trick against the Lions in a test match.

Van Vollenhoven, who touched down three times in the second test in 1965, went on to become a rugby league legend and Hall of Fame member, with only Billy Boston as competition for the title of the best player in the English game in the 1960s.

The other two players to score hat-tricks against the Lions are both All Blacks, wing Stu Wilson in the 38–6 fourth test drubbing in Auckland in 1983, and Frank Mitchinson in the third test 29–0 (equivalent of 47–0 in today's money) defeat of Boxer Harding's Anglo-Welsh side, also in Auckland, in 1908.

— TENTH TIME LUCKY —

Willie John McBride may be the most capped man in the history of the Lions, but he had more than his fair share of disappointment: his first win in a Lions shirt was in New Zealand in 1971, his tenth Lions test.

— LIONS RECORDS: MOST APPEARANCES IN TEST MATCHES —

For:

17	Willie-John McBride	1962–74
13	Dickie Jeeps	1955–62
11+1	Mike Gibson	1966–71
12	Graham Price	1977–83
10	Tony O'Reilly	1955–59
10	Rhys Williams	1955–59
10	Gareth Edwards	1968–74

Against:

11	Colin Meads	New Zealand	1959–71

— GREATEST LIONS XV: GERALD DAVIES (WING) —

Gerald Davies

Along with Barry John, Gareth Edwards and JPR Williams, Gerald Davies was one of four Welsh backs who captivated the rugby world in 1971. It was the greatest flowering of Welsh back talent since Percy Bush had spearheaded the first golden generation at the beginning of the century, and it was to blow away the All Blacks on their home patch.

The New Zealanders were, in fact, unlucky to meet Davies in such circumstances. On his first Lions tour, to South Africa in 1968, he had been injured and played just nine games. While he was the most creative back on that tour after Mike Gibson moved to fly-half to deputise for the injured Barry John, the centre was nowhere near the force he was to become after 1969 when he was pressed into action as a wing on tour in Australia and found his vocation.

Davies took 1970 off to concentrate on his finals at Cambridge, but the break seemed to completely reinvigorate him and when he re-emerged in 1971 he was on the wing and was a changed player. The searing pace, dazzling sidestep and sure hands that had served him well as a centre seemed enhanced on the wing, where he was a revelation. Davies was the dominant player of the 1971 Five Nations, scoring five tries as Wales won their first Grand Slam for over 20 years.

If anything, the stylish Davies ratcheted up the quality from there when he arrived in New Zealand. In his time there, he proved himself a devastating finisher with a knack of turning up on the end of flowing movements and of squeezing his way through seemingly non-existent openings for crucial tries.

It was Davies' late brace of tries in the second test that convinced the Lions that when they threw caution to the wind they could run the All Blacks into the ground. That is exactly what they did in the third test, with Davies himself opening the scoring with a typically opportunistic try after a bullocking Gareth Edwards' break down the blindside as the Lions beat the All Blacks 13–3 to ensure they could not lose the series.

Willie John McBride, recalling the day when Davies scored four sublime tries for the Lions in a violent and otherwise forgettable match against Hawkes Bay, said of the Welshman: "I've never seen anything like it in my life. He was the best wing threequarter I've seen. He had everything. He had pace, he had change of pace, he had sidesteps, he had swerves, he had hands, he had feet – he could do anything." Davies beat the following players (in order) to a place in the Lions Dream XV: David Duckham, Ken Jones, Peter Jackson, JJ Williams, Ieuan Evans and Rory Underwood.

Davies was appointed manager for the 2009 Lions tour to South Africa.

Gerald Davies stats
Born 7th February 1945
Tours: 1968 & 1971
Tests: 1968 SA 3; 1971 NZ 1, 2, 3, 4
46 caps for Wales
Clubs: Cardiff & London Welsh

— POLITICAL AMBITIONS —

The Welsh-speaking coach of the 1971 Lions, Carwyn James, stood as the Plaid Cymru candidate for Llanelli in 1971 and would have been unable to tour had he won. He lost, and the Lions won.

— 60 SCRUMS A DAY —

In 1974, both coach Syd Millar and captain Willie John McBride came from the small Ulster club of Ballymena and knew each other as only small town men can. Not only did they play their club rugby together, but they played for Ireland together and had toured South Africa together in 1962 and 1968. Both knew what awaited them and both knew how to confront the Springboks' reliance on raw power and intimidation.

Millar's response was to beef up the scrummage, which he did in some murderous 60-scrum sessions on arrival in Stillfontein. So intense was the pressure that English loosehead Fran Cotton eventually snapped and punched Scottish tighthead Sandy Carmichael. "We did 60 or 70 [scrums] a day, every day," wrote Cotton later. "I went out there 16st 12lb and came back close to 18st. My neck was 17in before and 19in after. None of my clothes fitted when I went home. That's how tough it was."

— TRY RECORD —

On the 1891 tour of South Africa, strapping 6ft 3in Blackheath and Cambridge University centre Randolph Littleton Aston scored 30 tries, including one in the first test and one in the third test, which remains a record for the number scored by any British player on a first-class tour to the southern hemisphere.

Aston's younger brother Ferdie was to be equally influential five years later. Living out in South Africa, Ferdie played for the Springboks against the Lions in the fourth test and put in the huge tackle on fullback Fred Byrne that dislodged the ball so that 'Biddy' Anderson could put stand-off Alf Larard away for what turned out to be the winning score.

— LIONS RECORDS: MOST PENALTY GOALS IN A TEST SERIES —

For:

PGs	Name	Venue	Tests	Year
13	Neil Jenkins	South Africa	3	1997
12	Gavin Hastings	New Zealand	3	1993
11	Tom Kiernan	South Africa	4	1968
8	Gavin Hastings	Australia	3	1989
7	Jonny Wilkinson	Australia	3	2001

Against:

PGs	Name	Country	Tests	Years
11	Matt Burke	Australia	2+1	2001
9	Don Clarke	New Zealand	4	1959
9	Allan Hewson	New Zealand	4	1983
8	Grant Fox	New Zealand	3	1993
8	Dan Carter	New Zealand	2	2005

— NIGTMARE FOR THE STATS MEN —

Interestingly there was no uniform scoring convention on the first Lions tour of 1888, leading to much confusion, then and now (for Lions historians and rugby stattos). In New Zealand it was one point for a try, two for the conversion and three for a goal. In the Southern Union (New South Wales) it was two for a try, three for a conversion and four for a drop goal. In Victoria it was one point for a try and three for any goal, whilst in the Northern Union (Queensland) it was one for a try, two for a goal and three for a drop goal.

— TINY TOMMY —

The smallest man to ever play a test against the Lions was Springbok scrum-half Tommy Gentles, who was just 5ft 3in tall and weighed only eight and a half stone.

— THE LIONS ON TOUR: 1971
(NEW ZEALAND & AUSTRALIA) —

In Australia: P2, W1, L1, Pts 25–27
In New Zealand: P24, W22, L1, D1, Pts 555–204
Tests: W9–3 (Dunedin), L12–22 (Christchurch), W13–3 (Wellington), D14–14 (Auckland)

The 1971 tour marked the beginning of the four most momentous years in Lions history. John Dawes's team was the first to return from New Zealand with a series win, and it was the first tour to have a coach who was given carte blanche to select the side and train it as he saw fit.

The man entrusted with beating an All Blacks side in transition was Carwyn James, the visionary Llanelli coach who was at the helm of the West Wales side which gave Brian Lochore's all-conquering All Blacks so many problems in 1967. James assembled a squad built around the Welsh Grand Slam-winning side of 1971, but the supporting cast was equally impressive.

Ten outstanding players – Barry John, Gareth Edwards, Mike Gibson, Gerald Davies, Bob Hiller, Rodger Arneil, Willie John McBride, John Pullin, John Taylor and Delme Thomas – had learned the harsh lessons of touring with the Lions in 1968, and were joined by talented backs like Dawes, David Duckham and JPR Williams, plus some of the best forwards the home unions have ever produced.

Barry John was the best of them all. He dominated proceedings, his faultless kicking keeping opponents on the back foot, and his deceptively languid running cutting unsuspecting defences to ribbons. Long before the end of the tour he attained superstar status and gained a nickname: 'the King'.

The Lions had a ball-winning pack and free-running backs, as they proved when beating Wellington 49–3 in the most complete Lions performance ever. Yet they didn't have it all their own way. Against Canterbury in what was thereafter referred to as the 'Game of Shame', violence flared and the Lions lost flanker John Hipwell and both first choice props, James's muse Ray McLoughlin and Sandy Carmichael, whose battered face was plastered across papers in Britain and New Zealand.

Nor did the Lions dominate the tests. The All Blacks had the better of the first test, and only some epic defence, Ian

McLauchlan's try and John's boot saved the day. The Lions were washed away by the black tide in Christchurch, but in the third test John was sublime, scoring a try, two conversions and a drop goal in the 13–3 victory.

The All Blacks needed to win the fourth and final test to level the series, and they probably deserved to win, but with the score at 11–11, the audacity and verve of the Lions was encapsulated by JPR Williams, who unleashed a 45-metre drop goal – one of only three he ever kicked – which was enough to see the game drawn and the series won.

Backs: Fullbacks: R Hiller (Harlequins and England), JPR Williams (Bridgend and Wales) Centres and wings: JC Bevan (Cardiff College of Education and Wales), AG Biggar (London Scottish and Scotland), TGR Davies (London Welsh and Wales), DJ Duckham (Coventry and England), SJ Dawes (London Welsh and Wales, capt), AJL Lewis (Ebbw Vale and Wales), CWW Rea (Headingley and Scotland), JS Spencer (Headingley and England) Fly-halves and scrum-halves: GO Edwards (Cardiff and Wales), CMH Gibson (North of Ireland and Ireland), R Hopkins (Maesteg and Wales), B John (Cardiff and Wales).
Forwards: RJ Arneill* (Leicester and Scotland), GL Brown (West of Scotland and Scotland), AB Carmichael (West of Scotland and Scotland), TM Davies (London Welsh and Wales), PJ Dixon (Harlequins and England), TG Evans* (London Welsh and Wales), ML Hipwell (Terenure College and Ireland), FAL Laidlaw (Melrose and Scotland), JF Lynch (St Mary's College and Ireland), WJ McBride (Ballymena and Ireland), J McLauchlan (Jordanhill College and Scotland), RJ McLoughlin (Blackrock College and Ireland), JV Pullin (Bristol and England), DL Quinnell (Llanelli), MG Roberts (London Welsh and Wales), JF Slattery (Univ College Dublin and Ireland), CB Stevens* (Harlequins and England), J Taylor (London Welsh and Wales), WD Thomas (Llanelli and Wales).
(* replacements)
Manager: Doug Smith. **Assistant:** Carwyn James

— LIONS RECORDS: MOST DROP GOALS IN A TEST SERIES —

For:

DGs	Name	Venue	Tests	Year
2	Phil Bennett	South Africa	4	1974
2	Barry John	New Zealand	4	1971
2	Percy Bush	Australia	3	1904

Against:

2	Macfarlane Herewini	New Zealand	4	1966

— 1974 APARTHEID CONTOVERSY —

The decision of the Lions to tour South Africa in 1974 was a highly contentious one. On the morning of the day on which the players were due to leave, anti-apartheid activist Peter Hain and 100 supporters invaded the Britannia Hotel in Heathrow where the players were waiting for that night's flight. The demonstration came after all other attempts to stop the tour had failed. Denis Howell, the Minister for Sport in Harold Wilson's government, had highlighted the abuses of John Vorster's regime, drawing attention to the fact that this was a man who had supported Hitler in World War II and had, according to Nelson Mandela, "escalated the fight against freedom to new heights of repression". Howell met John Tallent, the chairman of the Home Unions Committee, and pleaded with him to call the tour off, but it made no difference: the tour was going ahead.

When the protesters invaded the Britannia, the Lions were told at once. Captain Willie John McBride was angered, not just by Hain's group but by what he saw as the hypocrisy of the British government's support for the downtrodden in South Africa while it turned a blind eye to what he perceived as the injustices being perpetrated in his native Ulster.

"Willie John told us that if we couldn't cope with all this stuff, then the door was open," said Gordon Brown of the team meeting called by McBride. "He stood smoking his pipe for a good three minutes, making eye contact with each of us. Nobody moved an inch. He then walked across the room and kicked the door shut."

Not all the players were with McBride though. The openside flanker from the successful 1971 tour to New Zealand, John Taylor, was a shoo-in for the 1974 tour to South Africa. However, the

Welshman had toured South Africa in 1968 and seen apartheid at first hand and he not only refused to play the Springboks when they toured Britain in 1970 but refused to allow his name to go forward for the Lions. He also did his level best to persuade his flatmate Mervyn Davies not to tour either.

In the end, Gareth Edwards probably reflects the feelings of most of the players when it comes to the 1974 tour. In his autobiography, the chapter dealing with 1974 is titled, 'South Africa – A Thirty Year Quandary'. "Do I feel differently about going? Maybe my answer should be yes," he wrote. "Maybe I should feel contrite about having given some sort of succour to that evil regime, but if I'm totally honest I would say I am still not convinced I was wrong to go."

— LIONS RECORDS: MOST TRIES IN A TOURING GAME —

For:

6	David Duckham	v West Coast/Buller	16th Jun 1971
6	JJ Williams	v South West Districts	29th May 1974
5	Billy Wallace	v Griqualand West	19th Jul 1924
5	Peter Hordern	v Pacifico Railway AC	29th Jul 1936
5	Jimmy Unwin	v Buenos Aires FC	15th Jul 1936
5	Arthur Smith	v East Africa	28th Sep 1955
5	Andy Irvine	v Wanganui/King Country	1st Jun 1977
5	Jason Robinson	v Queensland Presidents' XV	12th Jun 2001
5	Shane Williams	v Manawatu	28th Jun 2005

Against:

3	Dave Cowper	v Victoria	13th Sep 1930
3	Tallie Broodryk	v Northern Province	13th Aug 1938

— MUSICAL TRIBUTE TO 'THE BOOT' —

Don 'the Boot' Clarke was such a legend in his homeland for his feats against the Lions that Don Catley and the Fernleafs recorded a hit song about him in 1965 called 'Big Bad Don'.

— GREATEST LIONS XV: TONY O'REILLY (WING) —

Tony O'Reilly

At 6ft 2in and 15 stone, with pace to burn plus a talent and thirst for scoring tries that comfortably exceeds that of any other winger in Lions history, flame-haired Irishman Tony O'Reilly remains the greatest Lions try-scorer of them all. The records he set in 1955 and 1959 remain in place today and are unlikely to ever be beaten.

O'Reilly was just 18 when he was first selected to tour South Africa with the Lions. He had only played five games for his club Old Belvedere when he was selected to play for Ireland, and had only won four caps for his country when the Lions came calling. The Irishman may have benefited from the management's decision not to take any players over 30, but he grabbed the opportunity when it came calling.

In South Africa in 1955, the teenage O'Reilly was a sensation and enjoyed the same sort of adulation that Barry John would receive in New Zealand in 1971. Not only was he scoring bucketloads of tries against the provinces, but his scores dominated the tests too. In the first played in front of 105,000 spectators and generally acknowledged to be the best Lions match of all time (see *The Greatest Lions Matches 3*, page 37), his barnstorming run made a try for back-rower Jim Greenwood, and then he latched onto a bouncing ball that had deceived fullback Jack van der Schyff to score what turned out to be the winning try.

When O'Reilly went over for the final try of the series in the fourth test, disclocating his shoulder in the process as a captivating series was drawn, he registered a record sixteenth try in just 15 games.

South Africa had given O'Reilly a taste for tries and he gorged himself in Australia and New Zealand on the 1959 tour. He scored two tries against the Wallabies and two more against the All Blacks, taking his tally to a record six test tries in ten tests. But out in the provinces he was even more prolific. At times it appeared as if he was unstoppable, the young Irishman scoring 22 tries to take his tally of Lions tries to 38, a record that still stands. So, too, does his record as the most capped Lions wing with 10 appearances to his name.

Witty, erudite and entertaining, if the outgoing O'Reilly was a natural Lions tourist, he unfortunately turned out to also be a stellar businessman. With his work commitments making the 1962 tour to South Africa an opportunity he would have to pass, his Lions career had effectively ended at the end of the 1959 tour, just a couple of months past his 23rd birthday.

O'Reilly beat the following players (in order) to a place in the Lions Dream XV: David Duckham, Ken Jones, Peter Jackson, JJ Williams, Ieuan Evans and Rory Underwood.

Tony O'Reilly stats
Born: 7th May 1936
Tours: 1955 & 1959
Tests: 1955 SA 1, 2, 3, 4; 1959 Aus 1, 2; 1959 NZ 1, 2, 3, 4
29 caps for Ireland, 1955–70
Club: Old Belvedere

— PHIL'S CAPTAINCY REGRET —

Phil Bennett was the compromise candidate for the captaincy of the 1977 'bad news tour' after the original choice, Mervyn Davies, suffered a brain haemorrhage while playing for Swansea in 1976, and the homesick Llanelli stand-off later admitted that in retrospect he should never have taken the job.

"I should never have accepted the captaincy of the 1977 Lions," he wrote after he retired. "I have spent many a wistful hour thinking of what may have been achieved had the leadership gone to someone far better equipped than I to deal with the all-encompassing pressures of a three-month rugby expedition. By the end of our tour in New Zealand I had no desire to stay in that country since I knew that all my weaknesses as a player and tourist were exposed in that short time."

— RUSTY IRON MIKE —

There was a definite split between some key English forwards and their Scottish counterparts on the 1989 Lions tour that stemmed mainly from a competition for places in the test team, but which left a legacy of bitterness. When Englishman Mike Teague dropped a ball in training, his Scottish rival John Jeffrey famously quipped that "it looks as if Iron Mike has gone a little rusty". That antipathy was in evidence at Murrayfield in the Grand Slam game of 1990 and by the time England played Australia in the 1991 World Cup final after a bad-tempered semi-final at Murrayfield, John Jeffrey, David Sole and Gavin Hastings turned up at Twickenham wearing kilts and Wallaby jerseys. Strangely, two of the fiercest competitors on that tour, skipper Finlay Calder and English hooker Brian Moore, forged a firm bond and remain close friends.

— LIONS' POINTS RECORD —

The 20 points scored by the Lions in the 20–9 second test win in 1993 remains the largest number of points they have ever scored against the All Blacks.

— THE LIONS ON TOUR: 1974 (SOUTH AFRICA) —

P22, W21, D1, Pts 729–207
Tests: W12–3 (Cape Town), W28–9 (Pretoria), W26–9 (Port Elizabeth), D13–13 (Johannesburg)

There has long been debate about which should be considered the greatest Lions team of all time, the 1971 or 1974 sides. It is a difficult question because where the class of '71 were a well-balanced running side, their 1974 successors ended the tour unbeaten and with a 3–0 record in the tests, largely by dint of the best pack of forwards ever to tour with the Lions.

Led by two uncompromising Ballymena Ulstermen in skipper Willie John McBride and coach Syd Millar, the 1974 Lions decided to target the opposing forwards, to smash them where their hosts felt they were at their strongest. They also agreed that they would never take a backward step, that they would never give in to the intimidation they expected to encounter. The result was the famous '99 Call' (see *The 99 Call*, page 31), the one-in all-in philosophy which led to some epic brawling, notably in the third test in Port Elizabeth, the notorious 'Battle of Boet Erasmus'.

Only two of the first-choice backs in 1974 had been in New Zealand, but five of the forwards had been on the 1971 tour, and it soon became clear where the strength in McBride's party lay. Yet the backs were no wallflowers, and once the forwards had subdued their opponents, players like Welsh halfbacks Gareth Edwards and Phil Bennett, fullback JPR Williams and wing Andy Irvine rammed home the advantage. They averaged five tries and over 30 points per match and scored ten tries to South Africa's one during the four tests. Their 97–0 thrashing of South West Districts at Mossel Bay remains the record defeat of a South African side.

Springbok skipper Hannes Marais reckoned the visitors an even better footballing side than Brian Lochore's 1970 All Blacks, and by the first test the South Africans knew what was coming. In the event, the Lions dominated but remained tryless and only won 12–3 in the mud of Cape Town's Newlands Stadium. They fixed that in the second test at Ellis Park, running the Springboks ragged on the hard ground of the high veldt, JJ Williams claiming two of the Lions' five tries as they won by the record margin of 28–9.

In the third test at Port Elizabeth the Boks surprisingly chose a No8, Gerrie Sonnekus, to play at scrum-half. Their coach Johannes

Claassen, under pressure to do whatever it took to win, had made seven changes before the second test and 11 before the third, and by the end of the series had used 33 players, 21 of them new caps, with only skipper Marais, wing Chris Pope and flanker Jan Ellis playing in all four matches. By the time of the third test there was only one option left to him – to fight fire with fire.

Sure enough, brawls broke out intermittently throughout the game, McBride twice using the 99 Call. The sight of JPR Williams running 50 yards to land a haymaker on gargantuan lock Moaner van Heerden's chin remains one of the most startling images in world rugby. Despite their new tactics, the Springboks still lost the Battle of Boet Erasmus 26–9 as JJ Williams claimed another brace of tries.

The fourth and final test was a classic. The South Africans had never been whitewashed before and were frantic to avoid the indignity. In the end, honours were even with a 13–13 draw, but even this match was not without controversy as first referee Max Baise wrongly awarded Roger Uttley a try before ruling out a perfectly legal match-winning score by Fergus Slattery on the grounds that he had already blown the whistle for full-time.

One remarkable statistic was that the Lions started three of the four tests with exactly the same side, and in the fourth made just one enforced change when lock Chris Ralston deputised for Gordon Brown. Here, for the record, is the side which tamed the Boks: JPR Williams; Andy Irvine, Ian McGeechan, Dick Milliken, JJ Williams; Phil Bennett, Gareth Edwards; Ian McLauchlan, Bobby Windsor, Fran Cotton, Gordon Brown, Willie-John McBride, Fergus Slattery, Roger Uttley, Mervyn Davies.

Backs: Fullbacks: AR Irvine (Heriot's FP and Scotland), JPR Williams (London Welsh and Wales) Centres and wings: RTE Bergiers (Llanelli and Wales), GW Evans (Coventry and England), TO Grace (St Mary's College and Ireland), IR McGeechan (Headingley and Scotland), RA Milliken (Bangor and Ireland), AJ Morley* (Bristol and England), CFW Rees (London Welsh and Wales), WCC Steele (Bedford, RAF and Scotland), JJ Williams (Llanelli and Wales) Fly-halves and scrum-halves: P Bennett (Llanelli and Wales), GO Edwards (Cardiff and Wales), CMH Gibson* (North of Ireland and Ireland), JJ Moloney (St Mary's College and Ireland), AGB Old (Leicester and England).
Forwards: GL Brown (West of Scotland and Scotland), MA Burton (Gloucester and England), AB Carmichael (West of Scotland and Scotland), FE Cotton (Coventry and England), TP David (Llanelli and

Wales), TM Davies (Swansea and Wales), KW Kennedy (London Irish and Ireland), WJ McBride (Ballymena and Ireland, capt), SA McKinney (Dungannon and Ireland), J McLaughlan (Jordanhill College and Scotland), A Neary (Broughton Park and England), CW Ralston (Richmond and England), AG Ripley (Rosslyn Park and England), JF Slattery (Blackrock College and Ireland), RM Uttley (Gosforth and England), RW Windsor (Pontypool and Wales).
(* replacements)
Manager: AG Thomas **Assistant manager/coach:** Syd Millar.

— LIONS RECORDS: MOST TRIES IN A TEST —

For:

Tries	Final score	Opponent	Date
5	24–3	v Australia (Sydney)	26nd Aug 1950
5	23–22	v South Africa (Johannesburg)	6th Aug 1955
5	24–3	v Australia (Sydney)	13th Jun 1959
5	31–0	v Australia (Brisbane)	4th Jun 1966
5	28–9	v South Africa (Pretoria)	22nd Jun 1974

Against:

9	0–29	v New Zealand (Auckland)	25th Jul 1908
7	5–32	v New Zealand (Dunedin)	6th Jun 1908
7	9–25	v South Africa (Cape Town)	20th Aug 1955
6	8–22	v New Zealand (Wellington)	9th Aug 1930
6	14–34	v South Africa (Bloemfontein)	25th Aug 1962
6	6–38	v New Zealand (Auckland)	16th Jul 1983

— JARMAN'S NOBLE SACRIFICE —

Harry Jarman must be one of the most courageous men ever to have played for the Lions. Having toured South Africa with the 1910 side and played in all three tests, the Newport second row rejoined Pontypool and in 1928 was at the Talywain Colliery, where he worked as a blacksmith, when he spotted a runaway railway wagon heading towards some children. Without thinking twice, he jumped in front of the wagon, derailing it and saving the children but sustaining such severe internal injuries that he died weeks later aged just 45.

— CONTROVERSY IN '93 —

The first test against the All Blacks in 1993 was notable for three hotly disputed decisions that effectively decided the result of the game. All three went against the Lions. The first occurred just a minute into the game when Ieuan Evans fielded a Grant Fox garryowen and was immediately tackled over the line by the All Blacks' former Samoan centre Frank Bunce. Although television replays showed that Evans never loosed his grip on the ball despite Bunce's attempts to wrest it from his grasp, Australian referee Brian Kinsey gave the try to New Zealand. Minutes later, Kinsey gave the Lions a penalty rather than a penalty try after Carling had been illegally held by openside Michael Jones as he attempted to take a try-scoring pass from Jerry Guscott. However, the most devastating decision came a minute from time when, with the Lions leading 18–17, the All Blacks were awarded a highly dubious penalty that Kinsey seemed at a complete loss to explain. Despite the Lions' continued protestations, the penalty stood and Grant Fox stepped up to give the hosts a win that perhaps should have gone the other way.

— LIONS RECORDS: MOST PENALTY GOALS IN A TEST SERIES —

For:

Pens	Name	Venue	Tests	Year
13	Neil Jenkins	South Africa	3	1997
12	Gavin Hastings	New Zealand	3	1993
11	Tom Kiernan	South Africa	4	1968
8	Gavin Hastings	Australia	3	1989
7	Jonny Wilkinson	Australia	3	2001

Against:

Pens	Name	Venue	Tests	Year
11	Matt Burke	Australia	2+1	2001
9	Don Clarke	New Zealand	4	1959
9	Allan Hewson	New Zealand	4	1983
8	Grant Fox	New Zealand	3	1993
8	Dan Carter	New Zealand	2	2005

— THE GREATEST LIONS MATCHES: 7 —

Australia 18, Lions 19
Third test
15th July 1989, Sydney

Not since 1899 had the Lions lost the first test and come back to win the series, but that's exactly what Finlay Calder's side did after being comprehensively outplayed in the opener in Sydney. In doing so, he became the first Lions captain since Willie John McBride to win a series.

The Lions had squared the series in Brisbane with some roughhouse play during a bad-tempered and often violent second test which became known as 'the Battle of Ballymore'. Despite the Australians' fervent belief that more of the same was in store for the series decider, the final encounter in Sydney was a clean game that was well won by a Lions side whose formidable pack crushed the life out of the Wallaby forwards.

But the third and final test will always be remembered for a calamitous mistake by Australia wing David Campese which effectively decided a very close series. The Wallaby legend fielded a miscued Rob Andrew drop goal attempt deep in his twenty-two, and pondered making a counter-attack before passing the ball infield to fullback Greg Martin. When it finally came, the pass was a wild one that Martin failed to hold and wing Ieuan Evans pounced on the loose ball for the converted try that put the Lions in front for the first time.

Earlier, despite being under the cosh up front, the Australians had taken the lead through an Ian Williams try and two Michael Lynagh penalties, while the Lions had three Gavin Hastings penalties to show for their labours. Ieuan Evans's try turned a 12–9 deficit into a 13–12 lead, and when Hastings added two more penalties, the Lions had a seven-point cushion to defend.

The Wallabies, however, displayed all the fighting qualities for which they are renowned, and dragged themselves back into the game with two Lynagh penalties to set up a frenetic final few minutes. The experienced Lions side weathered the storm, though, even if it was mighty close at times, to win by a single point. In doing so, they became one of only five Lions sides to have returned having won more tests than they lost from the 23 that have toured since the end of the 19th Century.

— THEY SAID IT 3 —

"We all aspire to play for our country as young kids but the Lions seem beyond us. It is only when you get into the international environment that you realise the ultimate accolade is to represent the Lions. And it is only when you become one that you understand the reputation of the Lions and why it has stood the test of time. I went to South Africa in 1968 on my first Lions tour as a 20-year-old and all they talked about was the tour of 1955 and a last-minute kick in Johannesburg for South Africa, which should have won the game for the Springboks but didn't. These are seminal moments in rugby folklore."
Gareth Edwards

"All champagne and travel."
Scottish centre **Peter Clauss's** verdict on the 1891 tour.

"Your top priority is not to win the tests in New Zealand, it is bringing the tradition of Lions play to Australia and New Zealand."
Unnamed Lions committee member to the Lions manager in 1966.

"Beyond learning the minor though petty and effective trick of feign-passing from Mr Haslam and learning to disregard the strict laws on offside play as regards the forwards in the scrum, I challenge anyone to tell me what else they [the Lions] taught us."
Tom Ellison, the grand old man of New Zealand rugby, on the 1888 tour.

"Once again the New Zealand forwards have saved the day by reverting to the type of play so necessary to football salvation. The whirlwind start of the British side was in painful contrast to their somewhat lame finish in the final test in Wellington, where their forwards were beaten decisively."
Geoff Alley on the 1930 series.

"While the Lions back division bristled with great names – some of the best in the world at the time – they failed to win a single test match. This suggests that forwards win matches, especially in New Zealand, and that the Lions pack of 1950 simply failed to match them."
Lions flanker **Clem Thomas** on the 1950 tour.

"New Zealand referees are not biased but they are not competent."
JBG Thomas on the 1959 tour.

"We all think that to some extent you people are quite mad. Though we may laugh and joke about it, we cannot fail to be impressed by the effect of a simple game like rugby upon a country like yours. Somehow we cannot express ourselves in the same way as you do, so we admire you for the enthusiasm you have for the game."
Alf Wilson, manager of the 1959 Lions to New Zealand, in his post-match speech after the first test.

"What I experienced in 1966 made a real impression on me. It shaped how I thought the game should be played, especially their passion for the game. I was coaching by the age of 24 and by 1967 I was taking squad sessions for Scotland and by then I was consciously modelling myself on forwards like Meads, Tremain and Lochore because I was so impressed by their speed to the ball, by their cohesion, by their tight-knit driving. Meads was the best rugby player I've ever seen. He revolutionised forward play, running with the ball, passing out of one hand, handing off players. But they all played simple, effective rugby and lived by the motto 'go forward'. I just copied them in every way I could. I played 23 of the 35 games on that tour and the rugby was relentlessly physical, with the country teams all softening us up for the All Blacks. Some games were just plain dirty. Canterbury was one, and against Auckland there were running fights all game, one involving 30 players. There was so much intimidation. They thought we were soft and they were right."
Jim Telfer on the 1966 tour to New Zealand.

"I would not describe today's game as dirty because all our games in New Zealand have been dirty."
Lions skipper for the day **Jim Telfer** at the post-match function after the Canterbury game in 1966.

"A nothing team."
Otago coaching legend **Vic Cavanagh** (the father of the ruck) on the 1966 Lions.

"I would rather die than go through such an experience again."
1966 Lions skipper **Mike Campbell-Lamerton** after the 20–3 first test defeat by New Zealand.

— THE LIONS ON TOUR: 1977
(NEW ZEALAND & FIJI) —

In New Zealand: P25, W21, L4, Pts 586–295
In Fiji: P1, L1, Pts 21–25
Tests: L12–16 (Wellington); W13–9 (Christchurch); L7–19 (Dunedin);
L 9–10 (Auckland)

This unhappy tour became known as the 'Bad News Tour', and it's certainly true that the Lions players were so miserable in New Zealand that they cheered when their plane home took off. Yet the tour in which the players developed a siege mentality and which is remembered in the popular memory as something of a disaster, was anything but. If anything, it should be rechristened the 'What If' tour.

Phil Bennett's side was stacked with prodigiously talented players, and while they were harrassed by tabloid journalists, depressed by the constant rain and saddled with a captain who didn't want the job and a coach who wasn't ready for it, it's also worth remembering that they remained unbeaten against the provinces (although the dirt-trackers lost to NZ Universities four days before the first test) and that they have only themselves to blame for not at least drawing a test series they lost 3–1.

The Lions had backs of real class and experience in Andy Irvine, Mike Gibson, Ian McGeechan, JJ Williams and Bennett himself, and their pack was so powerful that in the fourth test it reduced the All Blacks to the indignity of a three-man scrum. The front five of Fran Cotton, Peter Wheeler, Graham Price, Bill Beaumont and Gordon Brown was augmented by a back row of, among others, Welsh greats Terry Cobner and Derek Quinnell, and Irishman Willie Duggan.

In the first test in Wellington, the Lions were on top for most of the first half but had the wind knocked out of them before half-time by a disputed try from prop Brad Johnstone, which was followed shortly afterwards by a long-range interception try from Grant Batty which saw the tourists' heads visibly go down.

They lost that test 16–12 after a scoreless second half, but roared back to deservedly win a bad-tempered and occasionally violent second test in Christchurch by 13–9. Having squared the series, they were well-beaten in Dunedin where the All Blacks scored three tries in the first 15 minutes as the Lions missed six of their seven kicks at goal. Yet they could still have squared the series in Auckland.

How they didn't, losing 10–9 despite completely dominating up front, remains a mystery, but it was somehow fitting that it was homesick skipper Bennett whose missed touch led to Laurie Knight's winning try. Manager George Burrell summed up that final test when he said, "We outscrumaged, outjumped, out-everythinged them, yet still we lost."

So deflated were the party that when they stopped off in Suva on the return journey, they lost the test match against Fiji 25–21.

Later, the coach of that side, John Dawes, took responsibility for the series defeat: "The one big regret of my rugby career was 1977. It took a long time to get over it and move on with my life. I was convinced we had the squad to do a spectacular number on New Zealand – in fact I will go to my grave thinking that. [But] I wasn't quite ready as a Lions coach in 1977. It was too close to my playing days. I had successfully coached Wales after retiring as a player but the Lions is a bigger thing altogether. I hadn't quite served my apprenticeship for the biggest tour of all."

Backs: Fullbacks: BH Hay (Boroughmuir and Scotland), AR Irvine (Heriot's FP and Scotland) Centres and wings: DH Burcher (Newport and Wales), GL Evans (Newport and Wales), SP Fenwick (Bridgend and Wales), CMH Gibson (North of Ireland and Ireland), IR McGeechan (Headingley and Scotland), HE Rees (Neath), PJ Squires (Harrogate and England), DB Williams (Cardiff), JJ Williams (Llanelli and Wales) Fly-halves and scrum-halves: P Bennett (Llanelli and Wales, capt), JD Bevan (Aberavon and Wales), AD Lewis* (Cambridge Univ and London Welsh), DW Morgan (Stewart's Melville FP and Scotland).

Forwards: WB Beaumont* (Fylde and England), GL Brown (West of Scotland and Scotland), TJ Cobner (Pontypool and Wales), FE Cotton (Coventry and England), WP Duggan (Blackrock College and Ireland), TP Evans (Swansea and Wales), AG Faulkner* (Pontypool and Wales), NE Horton (Moseley and England), MI Keane (Lansdowne and Ireland), AJ Martin (Aberavon and Wales), A Neary (Broughton Park and England), PA Orr (Old Wesley and Ireland), G Price (Porthcawl and Wales), DL Quinnell (Llanelli and Wales), J Squire (Newport and Wales), PJ Wheeler (Leicester and England), C Williams (Aberavon and Wales), RW Windsor (Pontypool and Wales).

(* replacements)

Manager: G Burrell **Coach:** John Dawes.

— COACHES GALORE —

As well as 51 players, there were an incredible 29 back-up staff on the 2005 Lions tour of New Zealand. They included:

Bill Beaumont OBE: Tour manager
Sir Clive Woodward OBE: Head coach
Louise Ramsay MBE: Team manager
Andy Robinson: Coach
Eddie O'Sullivan: Coach
Ian McGeechan: Coach
Gareth Jenkins: Coach
Phil Larder: Coach
Mike Ford: Coach
Dave Alred: Coach
Dave Reddin: Fitness coach
Craig White: Fitness coach
David McHugh: Specialist advisor
Tony Biscombe: Video analyst
Gavin Scott: Video analyst
Dr James Robson: Head doctor
Dr Gary O'Driscoll: Doctor
Phil Pask: Physiotherapist
Stuart Barton: Physio/masseur
Bob Stewart: Physio/masseur
Richard Wegrzyk: Masseur
John Feehan: Chief executive
Richard Smith QC: Legal support
Louisa Cheetham: Media officer
Dave Campbell: Chef
Dave Tennison: Kit technician

— SOLE TEST TRIES —

In 27 tests, Kelso and Scotland wing Roger Baird never managed to score a try for his country – but he did get on the scoresheet for the British Lions, scoring in the third test loss in Dunedin in 1983.

Scottish second row Gordon Brown managed a similar feat. He never scored a try in 30 tests for Scotland, but scored in both the second and third tests in South Africa in 1974.

— ELEVEN ENGLISHMEN —

The record for the largest contingent from one nation in a Lions test line-up is 11, an occurrence that has taken place four times. Eleven Englishman appeared in the Lions starting line-up in two tests in 1889, as well as the second and third tests in New Zealand in 1993. There were ten Welshmen in the Lions team which beat Australia 19–6 in the first test in Sydney in 1950; eight Scots in the team which lost 17–0 to South Africa in the second test in 1924, and eight Irishmen in the team which beat South Africa 21–16 in the third test in 1938.

— SCOTTISH BOYCOTT —

The SRU refused to allow any Scottish players to travel to New Zealand with the 1908 Lions after a row over expenses when Dave Gallaher's 1905 All Black 'Originals' travelled to Edinburgh. Before the match, the ever-cautious SRU declined to cover the tourists' costs, which the New Zealanders had estimated to be £200, instead offering them the gate money, which it believed would be paltry for such an unknown side. However, with the Kiwis walloping established sides such as Devon, the match attracted much excitement and a full gate that November at Inverleith, with revenues of £1,200. The SRU was not amused.

— PHONE A FRIEND —

During the 1974 tour to South Africa, tour manager Alun Thomas angrily called a meeting to demand which Lion had charged £87 of telephone calls to his room. On receiving no reply, Thomas flourished what he thought was his trump card. "I have checked with the international operator and the calls were made to Newport 684210." Bobby Windsor, the only Gwent man on the trip, leapt to his feet and cried: "Okay, which one of you bastards has been phoning my wife?"

— MUD, GLORIOUS MUD —

The most famous rugby picture of all time is probably Colin Elsey's brilliant 'mudman' picture of Fran Cotton, taken when the 1977 Lions played the Junior All Blacks in Wellington. The picture accurately summed up a tour that was bedevilled by the worst weather New Zealand could throw at the tourists.

— LIONS DEFY PREDICTIONS —

Initially South Africa, the reigning world champions, were unimpressed by the 1997 Lions. Even after the Eastern Province Invitational XV, which contained five current or future Springboks and a Wallaby, were comprehensively beaten 39–11 in Port Elizabeth, their garrulous coach Johan Kluyts reckoned that not only was Neil Jenkins below test standard, but that the Lions would be beaten 3–0 in the series. In the event, Jenkins went on to score more points in a single series than any Lion before him, while the Lions had wrapped up the series by the end of the second test and only suffered one defeat on tour, a 35–30 reversal at the hands of the mighty Blue Bulls of Northern Transvaal.

— BOBSLEIGH BRIAN —

Brian Black, the South African who toured New Zealand with the Lions in 1950, went on to win two gold medals at the World Bobsleigh Championships in 1937. As well as claiming gold with Frederick McEvoy in the two-man event at Cortina in Italy, he also took gold when he linked up with McEvoy, David Looker and Charles Green at the four-man bob in St Moritz in Switzerland. A pilot, he met his death in the Second World War, perishing in the Battle of Britain in 1940.

— EAGLES IN CONSTANT FLIGHT —

Swinton forward Harry Eagles played every game on the 1888 tour – that's 35 rugby matches in five months and one week, plus 19 games of Aussie Rules Football, meaning three games each week. He stayed in New Zealand after the tour, playing for Wellington and Marlborough, and also touring Australia in 1893 as the senior player with the New Zealand national side. He returned to England in 1902, becoming a trainer to Dewsbury rugby league team.

— BODY DOUBLE —

Six foot ten inch Lions lock Martin Bayfield had a cameo role in the film *Harry Potter and the Chamber of Secrets*. Bayfield played a young Hagrid as he tried to save his young giant spider, Aragog.

— THE LIONS ON TOUR: 1980 (SOUTH AFRICA) —

P18, W15, L3, Pts 401–244
Tests: L22–26 (Cape Town), L19–26 (Bloemfontein), L10–12 (Port
Elizabeth), W17–13 (Pretoria)

Change was afoot in world rugby and this tour, which was opposed
by anti-apartheid groups and the British and Irish governments, was
to be the last tour to South Africa for 17 years. There were some
constants though, and once again a Lions tour arrived in the southern
hemisphere with high hopes, winning all of its provincial games
before coming up short in the test series, which Bill Beaumont's men
lost 3–1.

This was the first of the short tours, fitting 17 games into a ten-
week schedule, but it was even more notable for picking up more
injuries than any other Lions tour. By the end of it an incredible 15
replacements had joined the squad.

Most of the replacements were in the backs, with seven members
of the hugely competitive pack playing all four tests (Derek Quinnell's
injury saw Colm Tucker play the last two tests). Although Bruce Hay,
Andy Irvine, Ray Gravell and John Carleton all played three tests, the
back division was always chopping and changing and performed only
fitfully. With Terry Holmes, Ollie Campbell and Gareth Davies all
injured early on, not once did the same halfback combination play in
the tests.

If the Lions pack was good in the close-quarters exchanges, its
back row was sorely short of pace and Springbok openside Rob Louw
was able to get in about the halfbacks throughout the series. Although
South Africa were now effectively isolated and unable to tour, they
did have several top-quality players such as flanker and skipper Morne
Du Plessis, kicking fly-half Naas Botha, the incomparable centres Ray
Mordt and Danie Gerber, plus the old stager in the second row,
Moaner van Heerden.

Once again the Lions contrived to lose a series that was up for
grabs. In the first test, replacement stand-off Tony Ward kicked a
record 18 points only for Divan Serfontein's late try to give the
Springboks a 26–22 win. They were similarly close in the second
test in Bloemfontein, trailing by one point with less than ten minutes
to play only for the South Africans to score two tries to triumph
26–19. The bitterest pill came the third test in Port Elizabeth when,
in dire conditions, the Lions were in control and winning 10–6

through a Bruce Hay try, only for the tourists to be caught off guard with ten minutes to go by a quick line-out. Gerrie Germishuys slid over for a try that Botha converted to give the Springboks a 12–10 victory and a series win. Morne Du Plessis admitted that the better side had lost.

The Lions did, however, ensure they weren't whitewashed when they won the final test 17–13, coming from 13–7 down, with tries from Clive Williams, Andy Irvine and John O'Driscoll.

Backs: Fullbacks: BH Hay (Boroughmuir and Scotland), AR Irvine* (Heriot's FP and Scotland), RC O'Donnell (St Mary's College and Ireland) Centres and wings: J Carleton (Orrell and England), PW Dodge* (Leicester and England), RWR Gravell (Llanelli and Wales), PJ Morgan (Llanelli and Wales), HE Rees (Neath and Wales), JM Renwick (Hawick and Scotland), DS Richards (Swansea and Wales), MAC Slemen (Liverpool and England), CR Woodward (Leicester and England) Fly-halves and scrum-halves: SO Campbell (Old Belvedere and Ireland), WG Davies (Cardiff and Wales), TD Holmes (Cardiff and Wales), CS Patterson (Instonians and Ireland), JC Robbie* (Greystones and Ireland), SJ Smith* (Sale and England), AJP Ward* (Garryowen and Ireland).

Forwards: JR Beattie (Glasgow Accies and Scotland), WB Beaumont (Fylde and England, capt), PJ Blakeway (Gloucester and England), MJ Colclough (Angouleme and England), FE Cotton (Sale and England), SM Lane (Cardiff and Wales), AJ Martin (Aberavon and Wales), JB O'Driscoll (London Irish and Ireland), PA Orr* (Old Wesley and Ireland), AJ Phillips (Cardiff and Wales), G Price (Pontypool and Wales), DL Quinnell (Llanelli and Wales), J Squire (Pontypool and Wales), I Stephens* (Bridgend and Wales), AJ Tomes (Hawick and Scotland), CC Tucker (Shannon and Ireland), PJ Wheeler (Leicester and England), C Williams (Swansea and Wales), GP Williams* (Bridgend and Wales).

(* replacements)

Manager: Syd Millar **Assistant manager/coach:** Noel Murphy.

— OUTSIZED LION —

The biggest early Lion was English second row forward Froude 'Baby' Hancock of Blackheath and Somerset. When he toured South Africa with Bill Maclagan's Lions in 1891 aged 26, he was 6ft 5in and weighed in at 17st 2lbs – an astonishing size at that time. However, by the time Hancock came back to South Africa with Johnny Hammond's 1896 Lions, he had bloated to a remarkable 18st 8lbs. One newspaper of the time described him as, "the king of the line-out, but a real problem to fit into a scrum". He was fit though: he travelled from Wellington in Somerset to London each week to play for Blackheath and would often walk the final ten miles of his journey home.

— ALL-NIGHT PARTY —

In 1896, when the ship carrying Johnny Hammond's team arrived in Cape Town, it was too late at night to disembark. The South African players, officials and fans were so keen to greet them, however, that they chartered a tug at vast expense and went out to welcome their visitors. The South African party stayed on board all night, drinking, carousing and chatting until dawn, when they had breakfast with the Lions and then they all disembarked together.

— UTTLEY'S GREATEST XV —

Roger Uttley toured with the Lions as a player in 1974 and was Ian McGeechan's assistant in 1989, and few men have a wider breadth of knowledge of the Lions. This is the Englishman's Dream Lions XV: **JPR Williams; Gerald Davies, Mike Gibson, Jeremy Guscott, Rory Underwood; Phil Bennett, Gareth Edwards; Tom Smith, Keith Wood, Fran Cotton, Willie John McBride (capt), Martin Johnson, Roger Uttley, Fergus Slattery, Mervyn Davies.**

— DOBBO IS FIRST TO GO —

The first Lions player to be sent off in a major match was Newton Abbot, England and Lions forward Denys Dobson, who was dismissed for using obscene language while on tour in Australia with the 1904 Lions. The foul-mouthed Devonian was given his marching orders despite the efforts of Lions skipper 'Darkie' Bedell-Sivright, who first informed the referee that "Mr Dobson is an Oxford man and a gentleman" and then took his players off the field for 20 minutes in protest at the decision ("his huff arrived so he left in it" wrote one Kiwi journalist). Dobson was later killed by a charging rhino while working as a farmer in Nyasaland (modern day Malawi) in 1916.

The first Lions player to be dismissed for foul play was John O'Shea, who threw a punch after a last warning by the referee at the so-called 'Battle of Springs' in South Africa in 1968. O'Shea was pelted with fruit as he left the pitch and was then smacked in the face by a spectator, at which stage all of the Lions players, subs, non-playing reserves and management waded in. Willie John McBride gained the satisfaction of landing a solid right hook on the chin of the perpetrator, who was probably quite happy to be arrested shortly afterwards.

— ARGY BARGY —

While the 1910 Lions side were touring South Africa, another composite British side was in the southern hemisphere visiting Argentina. This one was led by England fullback John Raphael but included three Scots. Managed by Oxford University stalwart RV Stanley (of Major Stanley's XV fame), the 19-strong touring party won all six games comfortably, including the first test ever to be played by the River Plate RU (which later became the Argentina national side), which the Lions won 23–3 in Buenos Aires. The closest match was the first, a 19–13 win over Olimpicos A in Buenos Aires.

Then in early 1927, the River Plate Union asked the four home unions to send over a team and a 23-man party containing 11 internationals and captained by Scottish lock David McMyn duly arrived in Buenos Aires in July 1927 to play nine games, four of which were tests. Only CA San Isidro, who were beaten 14–10, put up any resistance, with the four tests being won by a points aggregate of 160–3. Yet the games were still packed out, leaving the hosts with a healthy cash surplus and an increased hunger for the game.

— THE LIONS TRUST —

In April 2002, Lions legend Syd Millar set up the Lions Trust, an organisation established to help any former Lions who meet with financial hardship as a result of serious injury or illness. The idea for the Trust came when he witnessed the hardship and illness suffered by Gordon Brown, the much-loved 1970s Lion who died of cancer in 2001. In addition to helping former Lions, the organisation will also raise money to fund charitable rugby projects in underprivileged communities. The Trust was launched with a dinner at which virtually every living Lions captain was present.

— OLYMPIC LIONS —

- Bim Baxter, the English international who went on to manage the 1930 Lions to New Zealand and caused huge offence by referring to the Kiwis' 2-3-2 scrum and rover as "cheating", was also an Olympian. He competed at the 1908 Olympics as a yachtsman.
- Cornishmen John Jackett and Maffer Davey, who were on the 1910 Anglo-Welsh team that toured New Zealand and Australia, went on to win Olympic Games silver medals in 1910. They were playing for Cornwall, that year's winners of the County Championship and therefore Great Britain's representatives. 'Great Britain' were defeated 32–3 by an Australia side including former Lion Tom 'Rusty' Richards' in the final (in fact the only game) of the London Olympics rugby tournament at the White City Stadium.
- Wales and Lions wing Ken Jones won a silver medal in the 4x100m at the 1948 Olympics in London.

— 'THE WRECKERS' —

The 1968 tour to South Africa was the first to be accompanied by a sizeable press contingent, one which also included tabloid reporters. It was they who took a great interest in the Lions' off-field activities, dubbing them 'the Wreckers'. The players, who caused tens of thousands of pounds worth of damage at the party after the third test, finally decided to see the funny side and formed an official club, The Loyal Order of the Wreckers.

— THE LIONS ON TOUR: 1983 (NEW ZEALAND) —

P18, W12, L6, Pts 478–276
Tests: L12–16 (Christchurch), L0–9 (Wellington), L8–15 (Dunedin),
L6–38 (Auckland)

If the unlucky 1980 Lions failed to get their just rewards when they
lost the series 3-1, Ciaran Fitzgerald's 1983 tourists could have no such
excuses. They performed well around the provinces, losing only to
powerhouses Canterbury and Auckland, but it was no surprise when
they emulated Mike Campbell-Lamerton's 1966 side and lost the test
series 4–0. The only thing that raised eyebrows was that the first three
tests were so close. They were, said coach Jim Telfer, "like lambs to
the slaughter".

As with Campbell-Lamerton, the choice of captain was a
controversial one which overshadowed the tour. Fitzgerald was a good
leader but was generally regarded as a weaker hooker than understudy
Colin Deans or Peter Wheeler, who was left at home. That belief was
shared by All Blacks skipper Andy Dalton. Yet unlike Campbell-
Lamerton, Fitzgerald and tour manager Willie John McBride refused
to countenance dropping him.

Team selection was a recurring theme on this tour, as was dirty
play, the usual injury toll and the fearsomely hectic match itinerary,
but all of those were incidentals: the fundamental problem was that
even though the Lions played with guts and passion, it wasn't enough
against this quality of opponent.

In theory the tourists possessed talented backs such as scrum-
half Roy Laidlaw, fly-halves Ollie Campbell and John Rutherford,
but they struggled to forge a cohesive back division. Their forwards
were competitive, especially tighthead Graham Price, lock Maurice
Colclough and breakaways Peter Winterbottom and Iain Paxton,
yet they were eclipsed by an All Black pack including top-quality
locks in Andy Haden and Gary Whetton, a back row of rare class
in 'Cowboy' Shaw, Jock Hobbs and Murray Mexted, all given
direction by arguably the best Kiwi scrum-half of them all, Dave
Loveridge.

Still, the first test at Lancaster Park was very close and there was
only a point in it when Allan Hewson smacked over a 45-metre drop
goal with seconds remaining to seal the 16–12 win. The Lions now
believed they could win the second test at windy Wellington, and
after the All Blacks only led 9–0 at half-time despite having a howling

gale at their backs, it looked as if they were right. But Loveridge marshalled his forwards superbly and the score didn't change after the interval.

The third test in arctic conditions in Dunedin was also close, and although the All Blacks won 15–8, the Lions took the laurels by scoring two tries to one. It was only in the final test when the All Blacks broke loose, scoring six tries to none as they routed the Lions 38–6.

Backs: Fullbacks: G Evans (Maesteg and Wales), WH Hare (Leicester and England), HP MacNeill (Oxford Univ and Ireland) Centres and wings: RA Ackerman (London Welsh and Wales), GRT Baird (Kelso and Scotland), J Carleton (Orrell and England), DG Irwin (Instonians and Ireland), MJ Kiernan (Dolphin and Ireland), TM Ringland (Ballymena and Ireland), CR Woodward (Leicester and England) Fly-halves and scrum-halves: SO Campbell (Old Belvedere and Ireland), TD Holmes (Cardiff and Wales), RJ Laidlaw (Jedforest and Scotland), ND Melville* (Wasps), JY Rutherford (Selkirk and Scotland), SJ Smith* (Sale and England).

Forwards: SJ Bainbridge (Gosforth and England), JR Beattie (Glasgow Accies and Scotland), SB Boyle (Gloucester and England), ET Butler* (Pontypool and Wales), JH Calder (Stewart's Melville FP and Scotland), MJ Colclough (Angouleme and England), CT Deans (Hawick and Scotland), CF Fitzgerald (St Mary's College and Ireland, captain), NC Jeavons* (Moseley and England), ST Jones (Pontypool and Wales), DG Lenihan* (Cork Constitution and Ireland), GAJ McLoughlin* (Shannon and Ireland), IG Milne (Heriot's FP and Scotland), RL Norster (Cardiff and Wales), JB O'Driscoll (London Irish and Ireland), IAM Paxton (Selkirk and Scotland), G Price (Pontypool and Wales), J Squire (Pontypool and Wales), I Stephens (Bridgend and Wales), PJ Winterbottom (Headingley and England). (* replacements)

Manager: WJ McBride **Assistant manager/coach:** JW Telfer.

— THE GREATEST LIONS MATCHES: 8 —

New Zealand 7, Lions 20
Second test
26th June 1993, Wellington

The second test at Lancaster Park in 1993 was the Lions' biggest ever win in New Zealand and breathed life into a series – and tour – that had looked like fading out with a whimper. It also ensured that Gavin Hastings' Lions avoided the whitewash endured by the tourists of 1966, 1983 and 2005.

It was a particularly significant and unexpected win because by the time the Lions arrived in Wellington for the second test, the tour was in dire danger of falling apart. The Lions' dirt-trackers had gone 'off tour' and were thrashed 29–17 by Hawke's Bay during the week of the second test. Even worse, the Lions had lost their last three Saturday games when they were beaten by Otago and Auckland before suffering a demoralising first test defeat which they felt had only been lost due to some highly contentious refereeing.

To make matters worse, Hastings had a strained hamstring and didn't feel well enough to play, and only some gentle persuasion from Will Carling and Jeremy Guscott at the behest of coach Ian McGeechan saw the Lions talisman finally agree to take the field as late as Friday afternoon.

Hastings and McGeechan had decided that they would play into the whistling wind and bright sun and try to contain the All Blacks before breaking loose in the second half, but instead Hastings himself lost a Grant Fox garryowen in the sun after half an hour and Eroni Clarke fell on the ball to score the opening try, with Fox converting. But with Martin Bayfield and Martin Johnson ruling the line-out and the Lions forwards in feisty form, Hastings kicked two first-half penalties and Rob Andrew dropped a goal to make the half-time score 9–7 to the Lions.

The second half was a masterclass from the Lions. They shut out the New Zealanders and for the first time in his test career Fox didn't kick a single penalty. The decisive score came from an All Black mistake when Sean Fitzpatrick spilled the ball on the Lions 10-metre line during a promising rolling maul, only to see Dewi Morris pick it up and feed Jeremy Guscott, who put on the afterburners to beat Frank Bunce and John Kirwan before offloading to Rory Underwood to dive spectacularly over the line. Hastings added another penalty to increase the margin of victory.

Fitzpatrick was inconsolable, calling it his worst performance in an All Black jersey, and the nation was incandescent, blaming the front five for what they regarded as an unexpected defeat of unacceptable proportions.

— LIONS BETWEEN THE STICKS —

- Irish-born Arthur Paul, the principal goal kicker of the 1888 team, was also a talented cricketer. Playing for Lancashire against Somerset in Taunton in 1895, he was Archie MacLaren's partner when he scored 424 runs in a single innings, which remains the English first-class batting record. A sporting renaissance man, he also played in goal for Blackburn Rovers Football Club.
- Andy Reed, the Bath and Scotland second row who toured New Zealand as a Lions dirt-tracker in 1993, was once a goalkeeper for non-league Bodmin Town.
- The great Gordon Brown played in goal for Ayrshire junior side Troon, and was the son of Jock, who played in goal for Scotland, Hibs, Dundee, Kilmarnock and Clyde, with whom he won the Scottish Cup in 1939.

— ABSOLUTELY EXCRUCIATING! —

In 1974, towards the end of one the notoriously ferocious scrummaging sessions in training, the test pack pushed the dirt-trackers' pack back and ran over the top of them leaving patrician Englishman Chris Ralston lying on the ground writhing in agony.

Irish hooker Ken Kennedy, who was also a doctor, quickly ran over to Ralston and asked him if he was okay. "Ehctually," said Ralston, sounding like Prince Charles, "the pain is absolutely excruciating." At which point the tour joker Bobby Windsor laughed. "You can't be in that much pain, boyo, if you can think of a ******* word like that," he quipped.

— THE LIONS ON TOUR: 1989 (AUSTRALIA) —

P12, W11, L1, Pts 360–192
Tests: L30–12 (Sydney); W19–12 (Brisbane); W19–18 (Sydney)

With South Africa off the touring agenda and the Wallaby Grand Slam tour of 1984 proving that the standard of play in Australia had increased dramatically, Finlay Calder's Lions undertook a dedicated 12-match tour of the country in 1989. It was the first time since Rev Matthew Mullineux's men played 21 matches in 1899 that a tour to Australia had not been combined with a visit to New Zealand.

There were other similarities with the 1899 tourists, most notably that both Calder and Mullineux's Lions lost the first test yet came back to win the series – the only two sides in Lions history to manage such a feat.

That first test loss was the 1989 Lions' only defeat on a tour that nonetheless provided them with plenty of hard games, even if some of the same opposing faces did crop up several times. It was a huge defeat by four tries to none as the Lions lost 30–12 in Sydney in a match in which their pack was comprehensively outplayed. Behind the pack the Wallaby halfbacks Nick Farr-Jones and Michael Lynagh operated in a comfort zone from which they completely controlled proceedings.

The fightback started against the ACT when the Lions found themselves 22–11 down at half-time. Only the application of forward muscle rescued the situation. It also pointed the way ahead for the second test, with Lions coaches Ian McGeechan and Roger Uttley drafting in Wade Dooley and Mike Teague, two of the gnarled English forwards who had beaten Australia 28–19 in Will Carling's first match as captain the previous year. The whole midfield was also reshaped, with Rob Andrew coming in at fly-half and Jeremy Guscott and Scott Hastings in the centres.

The Wallabies suspected the match might be physical and within minutes their suspicions were confirmed when Welsh scrum-half Robert Jones stepped on opposing skipper Farr-Jones' foot at a scrum, sparking an all-out brawl. The skirmishing continued throughout the game, interspersed with some cruel driving play from the dominant Lions forwards, for whom man of the series Teague was magnificent. Yet the Lions were still 12–6 down at half-time and it was only two late tries from Gavin Hastings and Guscott that saw the Lions win the Battle of Ballymore 19–12.

Despite a concerted campaign of media vilification of the Lions, the deciding test in Sydney (see *The Greatest Lions Matches 7*, page 119) contained none of the anticipated violence, although the Lions pack once again dominated. Instead, it is remembered for a moment of madness from one of the game's greats, Aussie wing David Campese. Penned in his own twenty-two by the touchline, he opted not to kick to touch and instead threw a speculative pass to Greg Martin, which the fullback dropped for Lions wing Ieuan Evans to gratefully pick up and plonk over the line. Two more penalties from Hastings gave the Lions a seven-point cushion and despite two late penalties from Lynagh, Calder's men hung on to win the match 19–18 and the series 2–1.

Backs: Fullbacks: PW Dods (Gala and Scotland), AG Hastings (London Scottish and Scotland) Centres and wings: JA Devereux (Bridgend and Wales), IC Evans (Llanelli and Wales), JC Guscott (Bath and England), MR Hall (Bridgend and Wales), S Hastings (Watsonians and Scotland), BJ Mullin (London Irish and Ireland), C Oti (Wasps and England), R Underwood (Leicester and RAF and England) Fly-halves and scrum-halves: CR Andrew* (Wasps and England), G Armstrong (Jedforest and Scotland), CM Chalmers (Melrose and Scotland), A Clement* (Swansea and Wales), PM Dean (St Mary's Colllege and Ireland), RN Jones (Swansea and Wales)

Forwards: PJ Ackford (Harlequins and England), F Calder (Stewart's Melville FP and Scotland, capt), GJ Chilcott (Bath and England), WA Dooley (Preston Grasshoppers and England), M Griffiths (Bridgend and Wales), J Jeffrey (Kelso and Scotland), DG Lenihan (Cork Constitution and Ireland), BC Moore (Nottingham and England), RL Norster (Cardiff and Wales), D Richards (Leicester and England), RA Robinson (Bath and England), SJ Smith (Ballymena and Ireland), DMB Sole (Edinburgh Accies and Scotland), MC Teague (Gloucester and England), DB White (London Scottish and Scotland), D Young (Cardiff and Wales)

Manager: DCT Rowlands **Coaches:** IR McGeechan and RM Uttley (* replacements)

— THE BRAINS TRUST —

The 1971 Lions team was the first to have a coach with full responsibilities while on tour (in 1966 and 1968 John Robins and Ronnie Dawson were called 'assistant manager' and had to defer to the captain, and even in 1971 the coach had no official hand in choosing the tour party). Once in New Zealand, coach Carwyn James enlisted the help of the players, convening the so-called 'Brains Trust' of garrulous Irish trio prop Ray McLoughlin, second row Willie John McBride and centre Mike Gibson to discuss decisions and selection. It was one of the strengths of the tour.

— WHIP-ROUND FOR BARRY —

When Barry John was selected to go on the 1968 Lions tour to South Africa, the inhabitants of his home village of Cefneithin were ecstatic. The announcement was made on a Saturday morning when he was on his way to Cardiff to play, and "by the time I got back to the local pub, the Dynevor Lodge, that Saturday night, I found the locals had collected £700 for me! Even a Mini car in those days only cost £820. You could buy a house for £3,000.

"They were so proud one of their own was to represent the Lions and wanted to make sure that if I wanted a new shirt, food or to have some laundry done, I had the money for that. I was a teacher at the time and they knew I was broke – like most teachers were then.

"Dear old Millie, who ran the pub, put a huge bottle on the bar and wouldn't even give anyone a drink until they had contributed. It was incredibly touching.

"By the time I was selected for the tour to New Zealand three years on, I was fully settled in Cardiff. But even then the villagers collected another £300 for me. It was almost as if they wouldn't believe I had left the area for Cardiff. Oh, he'll be back shortly, they were almost saying."

— COMPLETELY NEUTRAL —

The first Lions tour to have neutral referees was the 1980 tour to New Zealand.

— 'LIKE PLAYING ON THE SOUTH POLE' —

The third test in 1983 was played at Carisbrook in Dunedin, and it was so cold and wet that not only did both sets of players stay in the dressing room during the anthems, but All Blacks Stu Wilson, Steve Pokere and Allan Hewson (who had once previously been hospitalised with exposure at the same ground) all wore gloves to play. This was the first time any Kiwi players had done such a thing since the 1905 'Originals' tour of the UK in which several of Dave Gallaher's side wore mittens.

"I have never played in conditions like it," remembers Irish and Lions fly-half Ollie Campbell. "We might as well have played it on the South Pole itself. The New Zealanders were wearing wet suits under their jerseys, and they put plastic bags between their socks and their boots. We were all offered the wetsuits but I tried one on in the dressing-room beforehand and said no. The thing was we'd played in bad conditions before. I remember running out on the red carpet, stepping off onto the pitch and it was like putting your foot in a bucket of ice – five minutes: numb hands, numb feet, numb brain."

— RULE BRITANNIA —

The 1908 Anglo-Welsh team tried to come up with their own song to counter the All Blacks 'Haka'. This is the inspired effort that they eventually settled on:

Rule Britannia, Cymru am byth,
Rule Britannia, Cymru am byth,
Rule Britannia, Cymru am byth,
Hip! Hip! Hip! Hoorah!
Hip! Hip! Hip! Hoorah!
Hip! Hip! Hip! Hoorah!

— LIONS SKIPPERS —

Nine Irishmen, seven Englishmen, seven Scots and seven Welshmen have captained the Lions in their various incarnations over the years. Here's the complete list:

1888:	RL Seddon	England	(Australia and NZ)
1891:	Bill Maclagan	Scotland	(South Africa)
1896:	Johnny Hammond	England	(South Africa)
1899:	Rev Matthew Mullineux	England	(Australia)
1903:	Mark Morrison	Scotland	(South Africa)
1904:	Darkie Bedell-Sivright	Scotland	(Australia and NZ)
1908:	Boxer Harding	Wales	(Australia and NZ)
1910:	John Raphael	England	(Argentina)
1910:	Tom Smyth	Ireland	(South Africa)
1924:	Ronald Cove-Smith	England	(South Africa)
1927:	David MacMyn	Scotland	(Argentina)
1930:	Doug Prentice	England	(Australia and NZ)
1936:	Bernard Gadney	England	(Argentina)
1938:	Sam Walker	Ireland	(South Africa)
1950:	Dr Karl Mullen	Ireland	(Australia and NZ)
1955:	Robin Thompson	Ireland	(South Africa)
1959:	Ronnie Dawson	Ireland	(Australia and NZ)
1962:	Arthur Smith	Scotland	(South Africa)
1966:	Mike Campbell-Lamerton	Scotland	(Australia and NZ)
1968:	Tom Kiernan	Ireland	(South Africa)
1971:	John Dawes	Wales	(Australia and NZ)
1974:	Willie-John McBride	Ireland	(South Africa)
1977:	Phil Bennett	Wales	(New Zealand)
1980:	Bill Beaumont	England	(South Africa)
1983:	Ciaran Fitzgerald	Ireland	(New Zealand)
1989:	Finlay Calder	Scotland	(Australia)
1993:	Gavin Hastings	Scotland	(New Zealand)
1997:	Martin Johnson	England	(South Africa)
2001:	Martin Johnson	England	(Australia)
2005:	Brian O'Driscoll	Ireland	(New Zealand)

— THE LIONS ON TOUR: 1993 (NEW ZEALAND) —

P13, W7, L6, Pts 314–285
Tests: L18–20 (Christchurch), W20–7 (Wellington), L13–30
(Auckland)

The 1993 tour to New Zealand, captained by Scottish fullback Gavin Hastings and coached by his compatriot Ian McGeechan for a second time, was the last tour of the amateur era. It was also a tour of two halves: of a competent Saturday side that came close to winning the test series and of a midweek side that went off tour, leading to some embarrassingly heavy losses, especially against Hawke's Bay and John Mitchell's Waikato.

Despite a core of players based around the England side which had claimed back-to-back Grand Slams in 1991 and 1992 (17 of the 30-strong party were Englishmen), even the Saturday side struggled to impose itself in the early matches of the tour and in an ominous sign of things to come the test side was thrashed 37–24 by Stu Forster's Otago the weekend before the first test.

That was a disastrous weekend that saw line-out king Martin Bayfield stretchered off, Scott Hastings hospitalised with a broken cheekbone, Will Carling picking up a strained leg muscle and Wade Dooley travelling on the plane home after his father died. Yet if an All Blacks side in transition thought they could coast to a first test win, they were badly mistaken.

The first test started badly for the Lions when a Grant Fox garryowen in the first minute was claimed over the line by both Frank Bunce and Lions wing Ieuan Evans, only for Australian referee Brian Kinsey to award Bunce a try. Although Gavin Hastings kicked six penalties as the fired-up Lions edged 18–17 in front, worse was to come. Kinsey had already failed to give a clear penalty try, and in the dying seconds he awarded New Zealand a penalty for an offence which he has still to adequately explain. Fox kicked the penalty for a 20–18 win.

If the Lions let the test go begging at Lancaster Park, they made no such mistake in Wellington, winning 20–7 and putting in one of the best performances seen in New Zealand. The win was forged by their forwards but capped with a stunning try by Rory Underwood after a Jeremy Guscott break following a Sean Fitzpatrick fumble.

With the series squared, the stage was set for the deciding match at Auckland's Eden Park. The Lions led 10–0 after just 20 minutes through a Scott Gibbs try and a conversion and penalty from Hastings, but from there it was all one-way traffic as the All Blacks, keeping the ball in play to nullify the Lions' exceptional line-out, dominated completely, scoring three tries and relentlessly battering the Lions until they led 30–12 at the final whistle. So near but so far away – yet again.

Backs: Fullbacks: A Clement (Swansea and Wales), AG Hastings (Watsonians and Scotland, capt) Centres and wings: WDC Carling (Harlequins and England), VJG Cunningham* (St Mary's College and Ireland), IC Evans (Llanelli and Wales), IS Gibbs (Swansea and Wales), JC Guscott (Bath and England), S Hastings (Watsonians and Scotland), I Hunter (Northampton and England), R Underwood (Leicester and RAF and England), T Underwood (Leicester and England), RM Wallace* (Garryowen and Ireland) Fly-halves and scrum-halves: CR Andrew (Wasps and England), S Barnes (Bath and England), RN Jones (Swansea and Wales), CD Morris (Orrell and England), AD Nicol* (Dundee HS FP and Scotland).

Forwards: MC Bayfield (Northampton and England), AP Burnell (London Scottish and Scotland), BB Clarke (Bath and England), DF Cronin (London Scottish and Scotland), WA Dooley (Preston Grasshoppers and England), MJ Galwey (Shannon and Ireland), MO Johnson (Leicester and England), J Leonard (Harlequins and England), KS Milne (Heriot's FP and Scotland), BC Moore (Harlequins and England), NJ Popplewell (Greystones and Ireland), AI Reed (Bath and Scotland), D Richards (Leicester and England), MC Teague (Moseley and England), RE Webster (Swansea and Wales), PJ Winterbottom (Harlequins and England), PH Wright (Boroughmuir and Scotland).

(* replacements)

Manager: Geoff Cooke **Coach:** Ian McGeechan **Assistant coach:** Dick Best.

— THE GREATEST LIONS MATCHES: 9 —

South Africa 15, Lions 18
Second test
28th June 1997, Durban

The Lions arrived in South Africa unburdened by expectations, and even after an accomplished progress through the provinces and a 25–16 first test win that had climaxed with Matt Dawson's outrageous dummy and winning try, no one believed they could beat the Boks for a second time. South Africa's normally dependable fly-half Henry Honiball had kicked badly from the hand and for goal at Newlands – surely he couldn't be as bad again.

Honiball misfired just as badly in Durban, however, and was joined by stand-in placekickers Percy Montgomery and Andre Joubert as the Boks missed six kicks at goal. Yet for much of the match it didn't look as if it would matter. If South Africa's huge pack had failed to dominate in the first test, at King's Park they were unstoppable and relentlessly battered the beleaguered Lions pack.

Yet the Lions defence was heroic and indomitable, ensuring that South Africa were never allowed to pull out of sight. The Lions' back division showed as much invention and courage as its forwards showed grit. Gregor Townsend was always a threat from fly-half, and Jerry Guscott always threatened to ghost through midfield, while the bullocking centre Scott Gibbs put in an extraordinary performance of barely controlled aggression that famously culminated in him running over the top of 20-stone Bok prop Os 'the Ox' du Randt.

Even more than Gibbs and company, it was Welshman Neil Jenkins, playing out of position at fullback, who kept the Lions in touch. His pinpoint kicking saw him collect five penalties from five opportunities, two of them in the first half to put the Lions 6–0 up before Joost van der Westhuizen scored before the break. When Percy Montgomery added a second try after the break, South Africa moved ahead for the first time.

Yet despite scoring another try through Andre Joubert the Springboks could never kill off the Lions as Jenkins kicked all five of his penalty chances to level the scores at 15–15 with just five minutes to go.

As the Lions had roused themselves at the end of the first test, so they went on the offensive at the end of the second. Townsend took the ball up into the South African half but was buried under a pile of bodies, so Guscott stepped into his place and when the ball came back from the ruck he took one step and banged over a huge drop goal that remains the most breathtaking series-clincher in Lions history, beating even JPR's famous drop goal in 1971 for drama.

— ECLECTIC LIFE —

Outrageously pukka Scotland and Lions fullback Peter Kininmonth, one of the swashbuckling backs to whom the New Zealand public took a shine when he played in three tests there in 1950, led a highly eclectic life. Despite going to Sedbergh School, the alma mater of Wavell Wakefield, Will Carling and Will Greenwood, he didn't take up rugby until he went to Oxford University. Not only did he go on to become the High Sheriff of London, but at 79 he set up a cheese-making company, Cranborne Chase Cheese, that won numerous awards.

— DODGY DIET —

During the 1980 tour to South Africa, Fran Cotton suffered what was wrongly diagnosed as a heart attack during a match against the Proteas. It turned out to be an attack of pericarditis, an inflammation of the tissue around the heart, which the doctors blamed on too much red meat, fine wine and white bread. Cotton's reply: "Fine, I'll give up white bread then."

— DRIVING THE PM —

On the 1974 tour of South Africa, the Lions played a one off match against what was then Rhodesia (now Zimbabwe), beating them 42–6 before attending a dinner hosted by Prime Minister Ian Smith. After the dinner, and the worse for wear, Irishmen Fergus Slattery and Dick Milliken were leaving the reception when they spotted a smart black Bentley with tinted windows. As there was no-one around, they hopped into the car and were on their second circuit of the hotel grounds when the screen behind the front seats slid across and the prime minister stuck his face through the gap and said "Are you gentlemen looking for a job?"

— SUPERSTITIOUS LION —

The most superstitious Lions player of all time was an insanely talented Irishman called Rodney O'Donnell, who played in the 1980 tour to South Africa. In fact, the St Mary's College fullback was quite possibly the most superstitious man in the history of organised sport. A player so instinctive that he sometimes bordered on genius, O'Donnell had long been obsessed with the number 13. On the 13th day of the month O'Donnell would refuse point blank to leave his hotel room, and refused to enter any room whose digits could be combined to add up to 13. He even refused to stay next door to any such room.

The number 13 wasn't the only digit which frightened the life out of Rodders. Seven was another of his unlucky numbers, which is why he wore extremely tight 32-inch shorts (his real size, 34, added up to seven).

O'Donnell still blames 1980 Lions coach Noel Murphy for ending his career by insisting he wear a pair of size 34 shorts in the fourth test against South Africa in 1980, rather than his dirty, torn size 32s. His test career ground to an abrupt halt on that day, when he made the mistake of trying to tackle Junior Springbok centre Danie Gerber.

The savage back injury that finished O'Donnell's career when he was just 23 was two ruptured vertebrae – the sixth and the seventh (which added up to . . .). Gerber was, of course, wearing the number 13 shirt.

Even before his injury, O'Donnell's superstitions didn't end with numbers. He completely refused to walk on any lines, be they between paving stones, on the pavement or painted on the pitch. Fellow Lion John Beattie had the onerous task of sharing a room with O'Donnell on the 1980 tour, and remembers going out for a meal with the Irishman. "If you were walking beside him and he stepped on a crack in the pavement, he would end up hundreds of yards behind you as he retraced his steps," said the Scot.

O'Donnell's refusal to go onto the team bus unless he was allowed to go on last drove coach Noel Murphy mad, as did his refusal to leave the dressing room for a game unless he was the last man out. Unfortunately, the last-man-out-of-the-dressing-room superstition was an obsession shared by fellow Irish Lion Willie Duggan, with the result that one match in South Africa kicked off ten minutes late while both players tried to be the last one out onto the pitch. Duggan eventually gave in when he realised that it was either play with 13 men or let O'Donnell go last.

Once on the pitch O'Donnell had a strange set of actions before the game could begin, which included throwing the ball backwards through his own posts in the earnest belief that this would create a force field capable of repelling opposition penalties and conversions.

According to Beattie, however, that was nowhere near his most insane superstition – that occurred each evening when it was time to turn in. O'Donnell had a set routine that involved putting the phone on the hook "the right way round", fixing the curtains in a particular pattern and making sure all the pictures were at a certain angle, all of which would take at least quarter of an hour. "And then," said Beattie, "when he got into bed, he had to climb into it while touching the bottom sheet and the top sheet at exactly the same time. He would jump in until he got it right, and it would often take him 20 or 25 attempts before he managed it."

— MAKING UP THE NUMBERS —

In 1924, hard grounds, a small touring party and some ferocious tackling from their hosts meant that the Lions party touring South Africa had so few fit players that Irish international Bill Cunningham, who was at the time living in South Africa, was pulled onto the tour, the Lansdowne scrum-half scoring a try in the third test. In the town of East London a Scotsman identified only as 'McTavish' was pulled out of the stands and given a shirt to make up the numbers against Border. The Lions still won 12–3, although McTavish didn't make it onto the scoresheet.

— LIONS WIN, THEN SING —

The 1950 match between the Lions and the Maoris at Wellington was such a free-running, entertaining match that at the final whistle, with the Lions having won 14–9 thanks to the goal kicking of Lewis Jones, the crowd invaded the pitch and wouldn't let the players leave until they had given them a full round of *Auld Lang Syne* followed by *Now Is The Hour*.

— THE LIONS ON TOUR: 1997 (SOUTH AFRICA) —

P13, W11, L2, Pts 480–278
Tests: W25–16 (Cape Town), W18–15 (Durban), L16–35 (Johannesburg)

The 1997 tourists were the first Lions of the professional era and masterminded by Ian McGeechan, coaching his third Lions tour in succession, and his assistant coach and fellow Scot, Jim Telfer. In tandem with manager Fran Cotton, they plotted the downfall of the world champions in a tour that was as successful as Carwyn James's 1971 Lions, and just as unexpected.

McGeechan, Telfer and Cotton had all been Lions in South Africa and knew what to expect. They were masterful when it came to selection, both of the original party of 34 and of the test team. Few could argue with their choice of the highly respected England lock Martin Johnson as captain, but the inspired choice of six former union caps who had recently returned from rugby league took everyone by surprise. The idea was to inject some professionalism and discipline into the side, which was crucial on a short tour. Four of the six, all backs, played in the tests and all made crucial contributions.

More surprisingly for a short tour, there was genuine competition for test places, which made it an incredibly competitive party and goes some way to explaining why the Lions won all but one provincial game, a 35–30 loss to mighty Northern Transvaal the week before the first test. That there was rivalry for every position was proved by the selection of the test team, which included unheralded players like lock Jeremy Davidson and two props, Tom Smith and Paul Wallace, who were so much shorter than their Springbok counterparts that they completely negated the raw power advantage of their opponents.

A popular, happy tour off the park, on it the Lions had forwards like Lawrence Dallaglio, Keith Wood and Martin Johnson who ensured they were fiercely competitive. But it was in the backs that the Lions were at their best, with the ultra-physical straight lines of ex-league players like Scott Gibbs and Alan Tait contrasting with the guile of Gregor Townsend and Jerry Guscott, while scrum-half Matt Dawson kept the Springbok back row busy and Neil Jenkins, converted from fly-half to fullback, banged over goal kicks from every angle.

Although the Lions had impressed against provincial opposition, particularly when thrashing Currie Cup holders Natal 42–12, the Springboks were still stunned when they lost the first test at Newlands. The home side's forwards were on the front foot, but Jenkins converted every scrap of Lions pressure into points and then, with the score at 16–15 with ten minutes to go, Matt Dawson threw an outrageous dummy from the base of the scrum, sending three defenders the wrong way and allowing him to scamper over for the winning try, with Alan Tait adding another in injury time.

The anticipated fightback materialised in the second test at King's Park, Durban, when only heroic defence and five Jenkins penalties kept the Lions in contention. Yet despite being under the cosh for the whole game as South Africa scored three tries, Henry Honiball, Percy Montgomery and Andre Joubert missed six goal kicks between them and the two teams entered the dying minutes tied at 15–15. Somehow the Lions worked their way upfield and with seconds left Jeremy Guscott knocked over a towering drop goal to give the Lions an 18–15 win and a series victory. South Africa won the final test 35–16, but that was little comfort for a stunned home nation.

Backs: Fullbacks: NR Jenkins (Pontypridd and Wales), TGR Stimpson (Newcastle and England) Centres and wings: AG Bateman (Richmond and Wales), ND Beal (Northampton and England), J Bentley (Newcastle and England), IC Evans (Llanelli and Wales), IS Gibbs (Swansea and Wales), WJH Greenwood (Leicester and England), JC Guscott (Bath and England), AG Stanger* (Hawick and Scotland), AV Tait (Newcastle and Scotland), T Underwood (Newcastle and England) Fly-halves and scrum-halves: KPP Bracken* (Saracens and England), MJ Catt* (Bath and England), MJS Dawson (Northampton and England), PJ Grayson (Northampton and England), AS Healey (Leicester and England), R Howley (Cardiff and Wales), GPJ Townsend (Northampton and Scotland).

Forwards: NA Back (Leicester and England), LBN Dallaglio (Wasps and England), JW Davidson (London Irish and Ireland), AJ Diprose* (Saracens and England), RA Hill (Saracens and England), MO Johnson (Leicester and England, capt), J Leonard (Harlequins and England), ERP Miller (Leicester and Ireland), LS Quinnell (Richmond and Wales), NC Redman* (Bath and England), MP Regan (Bristol and England), TAK Rodber (Northampton and England), G Rowntree (Leicester and England), SD Shaw (Bristol and England), TJ Smith

(Watsonians and Scotland), RI Wainwright (Watsonians and Scotland), PS Wallace (Saracens and Ireland), GW Weir (Newcastle and Scotland), BH Williams (Neath and Wales), KGM Wood (Harlequins and Ireland), D Young (Cardiff and Wales).
(* replacements)
Manager: Fran Cotton **Coach:** Ian McGeechan **Assistant Coach:** Jim Telfer.

— TOUGHEST OPPONENTS —

Of the major provincial teams, Auckland have by far the best record against the Lions, having played them 15 times, beaten them on six occasions and drawn with them once. Here are results of the major provincial sides (and the Maoris) against the Lions since 1888:

Auckland (P15, W6, D1), Otago (P11, W5, D1), Canterbury (P12, W4), Transvaal (P16, W6, D1), Wellington (P10, W3, D1), Western Province (P15, W3, D2), New South Wales (P19, W3, D1), Griqualand West (P15, W4, D1), Northern Transvaal (P7, W2), Queensland (P13, W2), Orange Free State (P8, W1, D1), Eastern Province (P11, W2), Waikato (P6, W1), NZ Maori (P8, W1), Natal (P10, D1).

— STUDENTS MAKE THE GRADE —

When the Lions were beaten by Hawke's Bay 29–17 in 1993, both of the opposing second rows, who had been absolutely outstanding against the tourists, were English students on their gap years in New Zealand. Jim Fowler later went on to play for Newcastle while Bill Davison became a regular at Harlequins.

— EXCESS BAGGAGE —

When the 1955 team arrived at Zambia's Ndola airport to fly to Salisbury the total weight of the players plus luggage was too much for the plane to take off. Four players – Butterfield, Lloyd, Higgins and Smith – had to get off and catch the next flight the following day.

— GREATEST LIONS XV:
IAN McGEECHAN (COACH) —

Ian McGeechan

There is a case for saying that Ian McGeechan is the most successful Lion of all time. Not only was he a centre of rare quality who played four tests for the all-conquering Lions of 1974 and four tests for the under-achieving Lions who toured New Zealand in 1977, but he has also coached the Lions three times and been assistant coach once. The playing career and the successful stints as a Lions coach are almost certainly intertwined.

McGeechan knew the unique demands of touring with the Lions

from his days as a player, and knew the short tour format from his days coaching Scotland. He also knew the mentality of the New Zealanders, South Africans and Australians.

He employed that knowledge to devastating effect in 1989 when he coached the Lions under Scottish skipper Finlay Calder to a series win in Australia. McGeechan had coached Scotland against the Wallabies the year before, and he also knew that he would rely heavily on the English pack so he brought English forwards coach Roger Uttley with him and smashed the Wallaby forwards.

In 1993, McGeechan coached the Lions to New Zealand. Again he had a Scottish captain in Gavin Hastings, and again he relied on English forwards marshalled by the England forwards coach, Dick Best. But for a highly controversial penalty decision at the end of the first test, it would have worked. Instead a team that had been under pressure from beginning to end lost the series 2–1.

In 1997, McGeechan's Lions won a series victory over the Springboks against all the odds. With the help of forwards coach Jim Telfer and manager Fran Cotton, an imaginative selection policy up front and a tight focus on the demands of a short tour in the Veldt were the hallmarks of a famous and unlikely victory.

If McGeechan was part of the disappointment that was the 2005 tour, he can at least put up his hands and say that as one of four assistant coaches, it wasn't really his fault. When you've been as successful as McGeechan you're due a mulligan, a fact the Lions Committee implicitly accepted when they named him as coach for the 2009 tour to South Africa – his fourth time as coach.

So, McGeechan gets to coach the Lions Dream Team by dint of a consistent record of coaching overachieving Lions teams. By winning two of his three Lions tours, and doing so partly by choosing assistant coaches who could deal with the detail while he looked at the big picture, he is the man our side needs.

His forwards coach would be his old partner in crime Jim Telfer. No-one is more steeped in Lions lore, knows more about South Africa and New Zealand and is better able to motivate players; just go and watch the *Living with Lions* documentary account of the 1997 tour if you have any doubts. The backs coach would be Carwyn James, the Welsh genius who saw off the All Blacks. Finally, the manager would be Fran Cotton, the shrewd English prop who toured three times with the Lions and in 1997 was as entertaining and urbane a tour manager as he was effective.

— THE LIONS ON TOUR: 2001 (AUSTRALIA) —

P10, W7, L3, Pts 449–184
Tests: W29–13 (Brisbane), L14–35 (Melbourne), L23–29 (Sydney)

The 2001 Lions were groundbreakers. Not only were they the first Lions to be coached by someone from outside the British Isles in the form of Kiwi Graham Henry, and the first to be led by a two-times Lions captain in English lock Martin Johnson, but they were also the first to lose a series in Australia.

Although the Lions arrived as favourites and had 20,000 supporters in tow, the Wallabies were world champions, Bledisloe Cup holders and Tri-Nations champions, and had in Rod MacQueen and John Eales a coach and captain of unrivalled brilliance. Also, no British team had won in Australia since the Lions in 1989.

Henry and tour manager Donal Lenihan were determined to come back with a series win, but made the fatal mistake of deciding the test team on the plane over, so that the tour was undermined by a 'them and us' ethic virtually from day one. In addition, the focus on rugby was all-consuming and fractious players denied the usual social diversions of Lions tours simply got bored and stroppy. Two, Englishmen Austin Healey and Matt Dawson, penned critical newspaper columns that almost had them thrown off tour.

For all that, this was a formidable Lions team, possessing a pack that was built around a core of English forwards supplemented by Irishman Keith Wood, Scot Tom Smith and Welshman Scott Quinnell. They were to dominate the Wallaby forwards and provide a stream of possession for halfbacks Rob Howley and Jonny Wilkinson, as well as outside backs like the uncapped wing Jason Robinson and Irish centre Brian O'Driscoll.

That dominance was at its peak in the first test in Brisbane, when Robinson scooted over for a try within two minutes and the Lions forwards pounded the Wallabies into submission, Dafydd James, Quinnell and O'Driscoll all scoring further tries as the tourists won 29–13.

Yet MacQueen's Wallabies did not lack fight, and in the second test they found the key to the Lions. The tourists dominated the first half yet only led 11–6 at the break, but shortly into the second half Wallaby centre Nathan Grey took out Lions openside Richard Hill, leading with his elbow as he put the Englishman out of the tour. Only then did the Lions realise just how influential the quietly-spoken flanker was – his loss was the turning point of the game and the series. Suddenly the Lions started chasing the win and when a floated Wilkinson pass was intercepted by Joe Roff, things quickly fell apart, Roff claiming another try as Australia ran out comfortable 35–14 winners.

Australia rarely lose in Sydney and the Lions were by now suffering badly with injuries. However, the Wallabies only won the third test 29–23 after tries from Robinson and Wilkinson saw the game enter the final ten minutes tied at 23–23 before two Matt Burke penalties sealed the series win and rounded off one of the unhappier Lions tours.

Backs: Fullbacks: IR Balshaw (Bath and England), MB Perry (Bath and England) Centres and wings: MJ Catt (Bath and England), BC Cohen (Northampton and England), IS Gibbs* (Swansea and Wales), WJH Greenwood (Harlequins and England), RAJ Henderson (Wasps and Ireland), TG Howe* (Dungannon and Ireland), DR James (Llanelli and Wales), DD Luger (Saracens and England), BG O'Driscoll (Blackrock College and Ireland), JT Robinson (Sale and England), M Taylor (Swansea and Wales) Fly-halves and scrum-halves: MJS Dawson (Northampton and England), AS Healey (Leicester and England), R Howley (Cardiff and Wales), NR Jenkins (Cardiff and Wales), RJR O'Gara (Cork Constitution and Ireland), JP Wilkinson (Newcastle and England), AD Nicol* (Glasgow Caledonians and Scotland).

Forwards: NA Back (Leicester and England), GC Bulloch* (Glasgow Caledonians and Scotland), CL Charvis (Swansea and Wales), ME Corry* (Leicester and England), LBN Dallaglio (Wasps and England), JW Davidson (Castres and Ireland), PBT Greening (Wasps and England), DJ Grewcock (Saracens and England), RA Hill (Saracens and England), MO Johnson (captain, Leicester and England), J Leonard (Harlequins and England), RC McBryde (Llanelli and Wales), DR Morris (Swansea and Wales), S Murray (Saracens and Scotland), ME O' Kelly (St Mary's College and Ireland), LS Quinnell (Llanelli and Wales), TJ Smith (Brive and Scotland), SM Taylor (Edinburgh and Scotland), PJ Vickery (Gloucester and England), DP Wallace* (Garryowen and Ireland), DE West* (Leicester and England), M Williams (Cardiff and Wales), KGM Wood (Harlequins and Ireland), D Young (Cardiff and Wales).

(* replacements)

Manager: Donal Lenihan **Coach:** Graham Henry **Assistant coach:** Andy Robinson.

— WINDSOR'S WHEELS —

When the Lions returned from their triumphant tour of South Africa in 1974, Bobby Windsor got onto his bike and cycled to his work at the steelworks Gwent. When a local garage owner heard that Windsor couldn't afford to run a car, he considered it an affront to a national sporting icon so he rang the Welsh hooker and offered him a new car, for free. "He said he wanted to mark my Lions achievements and felt it was a disgrace that I was pedalling to work," said Windsor. Three days later, Windsor was forced to return the car or risk being banned as a professional.

— BLAIR DIES A HERO —

Blair Swannell, a tough Northampton forward who had toured Australia with Matthew Mullineux's 1899 side, emigrated to Australia in 1905 and won a single cap for the Wallabies against New Zealand that same year. He died heroically, leading a charge up the beach at Gallipoli on 25th April 1915.

— FRED SIDESTEPS BAN —

While in New Zealand with the 1908 Lions, manager George Harnett received a telegram from the RFU instructing him to send Cornishman Fred Jackson, the best forward in the side, back to England for alleged professionalism. Jackson had played for Leicester against the 1905 All Blacks and had, it was claimed, been paid for his efforts. He was also alleged to have signed as 'John Jones' and played for Swinton. Despite protesting his innocence, Jackson was banned. He never left New Zealand though, turning to league and playing for the New Zealand All Golds against England in 1910. His son Everard, who became a prominent Maori activist, also won six All Black caps as a prop in 1937 and 1938, but didn't play against the Lions.

— THE GREATEST LIONS MATCHES: 10 —

Australia 13, Lions 29
First test
30th June 2001, Brisbane

Two late tries for the Wallabies when the Lions were down to 14 men give this scoreline a sheen of respectability, but this was a good old-fashioned smash and grab by a Lions side which scorched out of the starting blocks against the world champions at the Gabba. Scoring four sparkling tries, the 29-point tally they amassed that night remains the second highest total ever posted by the Lions, eclipsed only by the 31–0 beating the 1966 Lions handed to the Wallabies.

The Wallabies had expected the Lions to try to strangle the game through a powerful pack led by skipper Martin Johnson and his lieutenants Keith Wood and Lawrence Dallaglio, but instead the Lions came out running, throwing the ball wide at every opportunity. The tone was set as early as the second minute when the ball was moved swiftly along the line from right to left, ending with Jason Robinson beating Chris Latham for pace and going over for the opening try of the series.

The tourists never looked back, with the pack's domination providing plenty of opportunities for the backs. None took greater advantage than Irish centre Brian O'Driscoll, whose searing break just before half-time put wing Dafydd James over, and whose virtuoso try just after the break effectively killed off the game as a contest. The result was put completely beyond doubt when centre Rob Henderson weaved his way through half of the Aussie back division to provide No8 Scott Quinnell with the fourth try, the coup de grace, to make it 29–3 just ten minutes into the second half.

As the raucous red-shirted hordes who made up 13,000 of the 38,000 spectators at the home of Queensland cricket (and virtually all the noise), saluted the Lions' victory, Wallaby fly-half Stephen Larkham neatly summed up the match. "We were ambushed," he said.

— CHERRY ON TOP —

The exceptional play of 22-year-old English loose forward 'Cherry' Pillman on the 1910 tour changed the way the South Africans played the game for the remainder of the century.

Although Pillman only played in two of the tests – and one of them at fly-half – he made a huge impression on his hosts who marvelled at his tactical genius. Pillman pioneered the position of the 'rover' or openside, where the 6ft 3in flier would detach himself from the scrum and use his startling speed off the mark to launch himself at the opposing fly-half. So successful was he in stopping their play that the South Africans followed his example, a decision that led to the tradition of openside play that produced Hennie Muller, Doug Hopwood and 'the Red Wrecker', Jan Ellis.

Billy Millar, the Springboks captain, was just one of the players who was in awe of Pillman. "The personality of one man crops up in my recollections of the game, and my memories of the game seem to be only of Pillman's outstanding brilliance. I assert confidently that if ever a man can have won a match through his own unorthodox and lone-handed efforts, it can be said of the inspired black-haired Pillman." Another leading critic said simply: "He played as if he had invented the game himself".

So skilful was Pillman that he won the second test virtually single-handedly while operating from the unaccustomed position of fly-half, setting up both his team's second-half tries and converting one of them. Had he been fit for the first test, then the tourists would certainly have come close to a series win. He underlined his virtuosity by ending the tour as the highest points scorer with 65 kicked points, despite having no record as a goal-kicker before the tour. His bravery was emphasised in World War I when he won a Military Cross.

— RED MIST —

The only player ever to be sent off against Lions was Duncan McRae for New South Wales in 2001.

— THE LIONS ON TOUR: 2005 (NEW ZEALAND) —

P11, W7, L4, Pts 328–220
Tests: L3–21 (Christchurch), L18–48 (Wellington), L19–38 (Auckland)

The 2005 Lions travelled to New Zealand at a time when the All Blacks were at one of their regular peaks and British and Irish rugby was in something of a post-World Cup trough. Even before they left, many struggled to envisage any combination of the players available to Clive Woodward winning a series against Tana Umaga's All Blacks in New Zealand. Few, however, expected the Lions to be on the wrong end of the most emphatic whitewash in their history, with all three tests lost and a points ratio of 107–40.

Just why the Lions were beaten so emphatically will be a subject of debate for many years. But with hindsight Woodward would probably take fewer players than the 44 and six replacements who eventually made the journey: with so many players on a relatively short tour, some players felt they had little chance to play their way into the test side. Many also wondered whether Woodward was right to place so much reliance upon the England team which won the 2003 World Cup but which came third in that year's Six Nations; when push came to shove, many of those Englishmen were simply too old or enduring a dip in form.

Not that there weren't high points. The Lions did dispatch provincial giants Canterbury, Wellington and Auckland, albeit sides shorn of their All Blacks, while Ian McGeechan's midweek side went through the tour unbeaten and posted the biggest win ever in New Zealand when they scored 17 tries in beating Manawatu 109–6. In fact, the Lions only lost one of the eight non-test matches, losing 19–13 to the Maoris for the first time.

Yet even more than Woodward's selection policy, the 2005 tour will be remembered for a piece of foul play which many felt skewed the series. The first test in Christchurch was just a minute old when a spear tackle from All Black skipper Umaga and hooker Keven Mealamu dislocated Lions skipper Brian O'Driscoll's shoulder and put him out of the tour. Not only was the distraught Irishman the Lions' best attacking weapon, he was also their defensive lynchpin.

After that, the All Blacks dominated every facet of play, with only the dire conditions keeping the score down to 21–3. The manner of the defeat and the controversy surrounding O'Driscoll's injury seemed to demoralise the Lions and give succour to the All Blacks, who went on to win the Wellington test 48–18 with young fly-half Dan Carter dominating, and the Auckland test 38–19, with Luke McAlister their main tormentor this time around.

Backs: Fullbacks: GEA Murphy (Leicester Tigers and Ireland), G Thomas (Toulouse and Wales), OJ Lewsey (Wasps and England), Jason Robinson (Sale Sharks and England) Centres and wings: MJ Cueto* (Sale Sharks and England), GM D'Arcy (Leinster and Ireland), WGH Greenwood (Harlequins and England), GL Henson (Neath-Swansea Ospreys and Wales), DA Hickie (Leinster and Ireland), SP Horgan (Leinster and Ireland), BG O'Driscoll (Leinster and Ireland, capt), TGL Shanklin (Cardiff Blues and Wales), OJ Smith (Leicester Tigers and England), SM Williams (Neath-Swansea Ospreys and Wales) Fly-halves and scrum-halves: GJ Cooper (Gwent Dragons and Wales), CP Cusiter (Borders and Scotland), MJS Dawson (Wasps and England), CC Hodgson (Sale Sharks and England), SM Jones (Clermont Auvergne and Wales), RGR O'Gara (Munster and Ireland), DJ Peel (Llanelli Scarlets and Wales), JP Wilkinson (Newcastle Falcons and England).

Forwards: NA Back (Leicester Tigers and England), GC Bulloch (Glasgow and Scotland), JS Byrne (Leinster and Ireland), BJ Cockbain* (Neath-Swansea Ospreys and Wales), ME Corry (Leicester Tigers and England), LBN Dallaglio (Wasps and England), SH Easterby* (Llanelli Scarlets and Ireland), DJ Grewcock (Bath and England), JJ Hayes (Munster and Ireland), RA Hill (Saracens and England), GD Jenkins (Cardiff Blues and Wales), RP Jones* (Neath-Swansea Ospreys and Wales), BJ Kay (Leicester Tigers and England), LW Moody (Leicester Tigers and England), DF O'Callaghan (Munster and Ireland), PJ O'Connell (Munster and Ireland), ME O'Kelly (Leinster and Ireland), MJ Owen (Gwent Dragons and Wales), G Rowntree (Leicester Tigers and England), SD Shaw* (Wasps and England), AJ Sheridan (Sale Sharks and England), MJH Stevens (Bath and England), SM Taylor (Edinburgh and Scotland), SG Thompson (Northampton Saints and England), AJ Titterrell (Sale Sharks and England), JM White (Leicester Tigers and England), JPR White* (Sale Sharks and Scotland), ME Williams (Cardiff Blues and Wales) (* replacements).

Manager: Bill Beaumont **Coach:** Clive Woodward **Assistant coaches:** Ian McGeechan, Andy Robinson, Gareth Jenkins, Eddie O'Sullivan.

— SKIPPER TAKES A BACK SEAT —

The skipper of the 1896 Lions to South Africa, Rev Matthew Mullineux, remains the only Lions captain never to be capped for his country. In fact, despite touring twice with the Lions and playing in the first test on both occasions, the Blackheath player was never even invited for an England trial. Mullineux didn't even play in the Varsity Match despite attending Cambridge University.

After the defeat in the first test for the 1899 Lions in Australia, Mullineux stood down and handed the captaincy to experienced English forward Frank Stout, whereupon the Lions won the remaining three tests. Although Mullineux was the first Lions captain to drop himself in the team's interests, he wasn't the last to do so. Other captains to have left themselves out of the test team due to lack of form include Doug Prentice (1930), Karl Mullen (1950) and Mike Campbell-Lamerton (1966).

— LIONS RECORDS:
MOST TRIES IN TOURING GAMES —

For:

Tries	Name		Games	Years
32	Tony O'Reilly		28	1955–59
28	Randolph Aston		16	1891
23	Jimmy Unwin		21	1936–38
22	Andrew Stoddart		27	1888
22	Mike Gibson		56	1966–77
19	Andy Irvine		29+5	1974–80

Against:

Tries	Name	Country	Games	Years
5	Morrie Collins	in New Zealand	3	1966–71
5	Tallie Broodryk	in South Africa	2	1938
4	F Unser	in South Africa	2	1910
4	Wally Labuschagne	in South Africa	2	1962

— FATHERS AND SONS —

There are four sets of fathers and sons to have toured with the Lions: Dubliner Jammie Clinch (1924) and his father Andrew (1896); Derek Quinnell (1971, 1977, 1980) and son Scott (1997, 2001), Irishman Keith Wood (1997, 2001) and his father Gordon (1959), and Scot Herbert Waddell (1924) and his son Gordon (1959). Amazingly, all four sets of fathers and sons to have played for the Lions played in roughly the same position: the Quinnells and Clinches in the back row, the Woods in the front row, the Waddells at fly-half or centre.

Those are not, however, the only familial bonds that tie when it comes to the Lions. Bev Risman (1959) was the son of the Great Britain rugby league team skipper Gus Risman, and also went on to play for Great Britain after moving to the 13-a-side game, while Barry John is also the brother-in-law of Derek Quinnell and Scott's uncle, and Tom Kiernan (1962, 1968) is the uncle of Michael Kiernan (1983).

— BRAVE AS LIONS —

Blair Mayne was not the only Irish Lion to distinguish himself in war (see *Blair Mayne: Man of Action*, page 24), nor indeed the first. Although he may not have been as much of a swashbuckling warrior as Mayne, Surgeon captain Tommy Crean comprehensively outdid his countryman by winning a Victoria Cross in the Boer War and then a Distinguished Service Order in World War I. The VC was for tending fallen comrades under heavy fire at Elandslaagte despite sustaining two life-threatening bullet wounds (the story goes that after the first wound he exclaimed, "I'm kilt entoirely" before realising that he could still walk, at which stage he jumped up and charged and took a fortified Boer position).

The larger-than-life Crean, who stood 6ft 2in and weighed in at 17 stone, won nine caps for Ireland between 1894 and 1896, his first three caps coming in the victories over England, Wales and Scotland which produced Ireland's first Triple Crown in 1894. He toured South Africa with Johnny Hammond's all-conquering Anglo-Irish Lions team of 1896, and did so alongside a teammate from the Wanderers club in Dublin, Major Robert Johnston.

The similarities between Crean and Johnston don't end there because not only were Crean and Johnston both Irish internationals playing out of Dublin Wanderers (Johnston won two caps for Ireland in 1893), but

Johnston also fought in the Boer War, was also a captain in the First Imperial Light Horse Brigade, and also won a VC. Just to finish off the remarkably similar paths their lives took, both Crean and Johnston emigrated to South Africa and went on to play for Transvaal.

Incredibly three of the four VCs to be given to rugby internationals have gone to players from Dublin Wanderers. The third went to Frederick Harvey, who collected his VC for single-handedly capturing a machine-gun post on horseback on the Western Front during World War I. Although Welshman Sir Tasker Watkins remains the best known rugby VC (despite being president of the Welsh Rugby Union he was not an international), the other rugby VC went to Arthur Harris of United Services Portsmouth. In all, 203 rugby internationals from the seven 'allied' nations have been decorated during wartime, including Crean and Johnston's 1896 teammate, Rev Matthew Mullieux, who went on to captain the 1899 team: he won an MC for his religious ministry under fire in France in World War I.

— MINING A RICH SEAM —

When the Lions first visited South Africa in 1891, the weakest opposition they faced was in Eastern Province and on the High Veldt, where they put 46 points past Transvaal and conceded none. However, by the time Mark Morrison's men returned in 1903, they found that Transvaal and Northern Transvaal provided some of the toughest games on tour, with Transvaal gaining the distinction of becoming the only provincial side ever to beat the Lions twice on the same tour. One of the main reasons for this was the influx of New Zealanders and Australians to work in the mining industry in the area – the Northern Transvaal side of 1903 contained no fewer than six Kiwis.

— FIRST SUB —

Mike Gibson became the first player from the British Isles to win a cap as a replacement when he came on for Barry John in the opening test of the 1968 Lions tour of South Africa.

— OFFICIAL TEST RESULTS: 1891–2005 —

Test	Team name	Date	Opponents	Venue	Result
1	Great Britain	30 Jul 1891	South Africa	Port Elizabeth	Won 4–0
2	Great Britain	29 Aug 1891	South Africa	Kimberley	Won 3–0
3	Great Britain	5 Seo 1891	South Africa	Cape Town	Won 4–0
4	Great Britain	30 Jul 1896	South Africa	Port Elizabeth	Won 8–0
5	Great Britain	22 Aug 1896	South Africa	Johannesburg	Won 17–8
6	Great Britain	29 Aug 1896	South Africa	Kimberley	Won 9–3
7	Great Britain	5 Sep 1896	South Africa	Cape Town	Lost 0–5
8	Great Britain	24 Jun 1899	Australia	Sydney	Lost 3–13
9	Great Britain	22 Jul 1899	Australia	Brisbane	Won 11–0
10	Great Britain	5 Aug 1899	Australia	Sydney	Won 11–10
11	Great Britain	12 Aug 1899	Australia	Sydney	Won 13–0
12	Great Britain	26 Aug 1903	South Africa	Johannesburg	Drew 10–10
13	Great Britain	5 Sep 1903	South Africa	Kimberley	Drew 0–0
14	Great Britain	12 Sep 1903	South Africa	Cape Town	Lost 0–8
15	Great Britain	2 Jul 1904	Australia	Sydney	Won 17–0
16	Great Britain	23 Jul 1904	Australia	Brisbane	Won 17–3
17	Great Britain	30 Jul 1904	Australia	Sydney	Won 16–0
18	Great Britain	13 Aug 1904	New Zealand	Wellington	Lost 3–9
19	Anglo–Welsh	6 Jun 1908	New Zealand	Dunedin	Lost 5–32
20	Anglo–Welsh	27 Jun 1908	New Zealand	Wellington	Drew 3–3
21	Anglo–Welsh	25 Jul 1908	New Zealand	Auckland	Lost 0–29
22	Great Britain	6 Aug 1910	South Africa	Johannesburg	Lost 10–14
23	Great Britain	27 Aug 1910	South Africa	Port Elizabeth	Won 8–3
24	Great Britain	3 Sep 1910	South Africa	Cape Town	Lost 5–21
25	Great Britain	16 Aug 1924	South Africa	Durban	Lost 3–7
26	Great Britain	23 Aug 1924	South Africa	Johannesburg	Lost 0–17
27	Great Britain	13 Sep 1924	South Africa	Port Elizabeth	Drew 3–3
28	Great Britain	20 Sep 1924	South Africa	Cape Town	Lost 9–16
29	Great Britain	21 Jun 1930	New Zealand	Dunedin	Won 6–3
30	Great Britain	5 Jul 1930	New Zealand	Christchurch	Lost 10–13
31	Great Britain	26 Jul 1930	New Zealand	Auckland	Lost 10–15
32	Great Britain	9 Aug 1930	New Zealand	Wellington	Lost 8–22
33	Great Britain	30 Aug 1930	Australia	Sydney	Lost 5–6
34	British Isles	6 Aug 1938	South Africa	Johannesburg	Lost 12–26
35	British Isles	3 Sep 1938	South Africa	Port Elizabeth	Lost 3–19
36	British Isles	10 Sep 1938	South Africa	Cape Town	Won 21–16
37	British Isles	27 May 1950	New Zealand	Dunedin	Drew 9–9
38	British Isles	10 Jun 1950	New Zealand	Christchurch	Lost 0–8
39	British Isles	1 Jul 1950	New Zealand	Wellington	Lost 3–6
40	British Isles	29 Jul 1950	New Zealand	Auckland	Lost 8–11

41	British Isles	19 Aug 1950	Australia	Brisbane	Won 19–6
42	British Isles	26 Aug 1950	Australia	Sydney	Won 24–3
43	British Isles	6 Aug 1955	South Africa	Johannesburg	Won 23–22
44	British Isles	20 Aug 1955	South Africa	Cape Town	Lost 9–25
45	British Isles	3 Sep 1955	South Africa	Pretoria	Won 9–6
46	British Isles	24 Sep 1955	South Africa	Port Elizabeth	Lost 8–22
47	British Isles	6 Jun 1959	Australia	Brisbane	Won 17–6
48	British Isles	13 Jun 1959	Australia	Sydney	Won 24–3
49	British Isles	18 Jul 1959	New Zealand	Dunedin	Lost 17–18
50	British Isles	15 Aug 1959	New Zealand	Wellington	Lost 8–11
51	British Isles	29 Aug 1959	New Zealand	Christchurch	Lost 8–22
52	British Isles	19 Sep 1959	New Zealand	Auckland	Won 9–6
53	British Isles	23 Jun 1962	South Africa	Johannesburg	Drew 3–3
54	British Isles	21 Jul 1962	South Africa	Durban	Lost 0–3
55	British Isles	4 Aug 1962	South Africa	Cape Town	Lost 3–8
56	British Isles	25 Aug 1962	South Africa	Bloemfontein	Lost 14–34
57	British Isles	28 May 1966	Australia	Sydney	Won 11–8
58	British Isles	4 Jun 1966	Australia	Brisbane	Won 31–0
59	British Isles	16 Jul 1966	New Zealand	Dunedin	Lost 3–20
60	British Isles	6 Aug 1966	New Zealand	Wellington	Lost 12–16
61	British Isles	27 Aug 1966	New Zealand	Christchurch	Lost 6–19
62	British Isles	10 Sep 1966	New Zealand	Auckland	Lost 11–24
63	British Isles	8 Jun 1968	South Africa	Pretoria	Lost 20–25
64	British Isles	22 Jun 1968	South Africa	Port Elizabeth	Drew 6–6
65	British Isles	13 Jul 1968	South Africa	Cape Town	Lost 6–11
66	British Isles	27 Jul 1968	South Africa	Johannesburg	Lost 6–19
67	British Isles	26 Jun 1971	New Zealand	Dunedin	Won 9–3
68	British Isles	10 Jul 1971	New Zealand	Christchurch	Lost 12–22
69	British Isles	31 Jul 1971	New Zealand	Wellington	Won 13–3
70	British Isles	14 Aug 1971	New Zealand	Auckland	Drew 14–14
71	British Isles	8 Jun 1974	South Africa	Cape Town	Won 12–3
72	British Isles	22 Jun 1974	South Africa	Pretoria	Won 28–9
73	British Isles	13 Jul 1974	South Africa	Port Elizabeth	Won 26–9
74	British Isles	27 Jul 1974	South Africa	Johannesburg	Drew 13–13
75	British Isles	18 Jun 1977	New Zealand	Wellington	Lost 12–16
76	British Isles	9 Jul 1977	New Zealand	Christchurch	Won 13–9
77	British Isles	30 Jul 1977	New Zealand	Dunedin	Lost 7–19
78	British Isles	13 Aug 1977	New Zealand	Auckland	Lost 9–10
79	British Isles	31 May 1980	South Africa	Cape Town	Lost 22–26
80	British Isles	14 Jun 1980	South Africa	Bloemfontein	Lost 19–26
81	British Isles	28 Jun 1980	South Africa	Port Elizabeth	Lost 10–12
82	British Isles	12 Jul 1980	South Africa	Pretoria	Won 17–13

83	British Isles	4 Jun 1983	New Zealand	Christchurch	Lost 12–16
84	British Isles	18 Jun 1983	New Zealand	Wellington	Lost 0–9
85	British Isles	2 Jul 1983	New Zealand	Dunedin	Lost 8–15
86	British Isles	16 Jul 1983	New Zealand	Auckland	Lost 6–38
87	British Isles	1 Jul 1989	Australia	Sydney	Lost 12–30
88	British Isles	8 Jul 1989	Australia	Brisbane	Won 19–12
89	British Isles	15 Jul 1989	Australia	Sydney	Won 19–18
90	British Isles	12 Jun 1993	New Zealand	Christchurch	Lost 18–20
91	British Isles	26 Jun 1993	New Zealand	Wellington	Won 20–7
92	British Isles	3 Jul 1993	New Zealand	Auckland	Lost 13–30
93	British Isles	21 Jun 1997	South Africa	Cape Town	Won 25–16
94	British Isles	28 Jun 1997	South Africa	Durban	Won 18–15
95	British Isles	5 Jul 1997	South Africa	Johannesburg	Lost 16–35
96	British & Irish Lions	30 Jun 2001	Australia	Brisbane	Won 29–13
97	British & Irish Lions	7 Jul 2001	Australia	Melbourne	Lost 14–35
98	British & Irish Lions	14 Jul 2001	Australia	Sydney	Lost 23–29
99	British & Irish Lions	23 May 2005	Argentina	Cardiff	Drew 25–25
100	British & Irish Lions	25 Jun 2005	New Zealand	Christchurch	Lost 3–21
101	British & Irish Lions	2 Jul 2005	New Zealand	Wellington	Lost 18–48
102	British & Irish Lions	9 Jul 2005	New Zealand	Auckland	Lost 19–38

— 2009 SOUTH AFRICA TOUR SCHEDULE —

Saturday 30th May
v Highfield XV
(Royal Bafokeng Stadium, Rustenburg)

Wednesday 3rd June
v Gauteng Golden Lions
(Ellis Park, Johannesburg)

Saturday 6th June
v Free State Cheetahs
(Vodacom Park, Blomfontein)

Wednesday 10th June
Natal Sharks
(ABSA Stadium, Durban)

Saturday 13th June
v Western Province
(Newlands, Cape Town)

Monday or Tuesday 15/16th June (TBC)
v Coastal XV
(Port Elizabeth)

Saturday 20th June
v South Africa, First Test
(ABSA Stadium, Durban)

Tuesday 23rd June
Emerging Springboks
(Newlands, Cape Town)

Saturday 27th June
v South Africa, Second Test
(Loftus Versfeld, Pretoria)

Saturday 4th July
v South Africa, Third Test
(Ellis Park, Johannesburg)